The Wiersbe
BIBLE STUDY SERIES

The
Wiersbe
BIBLE STUDY SERIES

2 KINGS & 2 CHRONICLES

Standing

Firmly

against the

World's Tides

David C Cook®
transforming lives together

THE WIERSBE BIBLE STUDY SERIES: 2 KINGS & 2 CHRONICLES
Published by David C Cook
4050 Lee Vance View
Colorado Springs, CO 80918 U.S.A.

David C Cook Distribution Canada
55 Woodslee Avenue, Paris, Ontario, Canada N3L 3E5

David C Cook U.K., Kingsway Communications
Eastbourne, East Sussex BN23 6NT, England

The graphic circle C logo is a registered trademark of David C Cook.

All excerpts taken from *Be Distinct*, second edition, published by David C
Cook © 2010 Warren W. Wiersbe, ISBN 978-1-4347-0051-3.

ISBN 978-1-4347-0698-0
eISBN 978-0-7814-1362-6

The Team: Steve Parolini, Karen Lee-Thorp, Amy Konyndyk,
Nick Lee, Jack Campbell, Channing Brooks, Karen Athen
Series Cover Design: John Hamilton Design
Cover Photo: iStockphoto

Printed in the United States of America
First Edition 2015

1 2 3 4 5 6 7 8 9 10

082815

Contents

Introduction to 2 Kings and 2 Chronicles

A Way Through

"The Christian life is not a way out of life but a way through life," said evangelist Billy Graham. God doesn't save us and hide us away until He takes us to heaven. He saves us and then drops us in the midst of difficult situations and challenges, and He expects us to make a difference.

The book of 2 Kings describes what happens to a people when the conformers take over. It records the end of the northern kingdom of Samaria, when the Assyrians seized power, and the captivity of the southern kingdom of Judah by the Babylonians. The book of 2 Chronicles parallels 2 Kings, and we shall consider it as we go along.

A Distinctive Message

Both kingdoms rebelled against the covenant of the Lord and became like the idolatrous nations around them. Many of the kings of Judah followed the examples of Jeroboam and Ahab instead of the example of David. God sent His messengers to call His people back to His Word, men including Elijah and Elisha as well as the kings Jehoash, Hezekiah, and Josiah. "But they mocked God's messengers, despised his words and scoffed at his prophets until the wrath of the LORD was aroused against his people and there was no remedy" (2 Chron. 36:16).

When society around us is in moral and spiritual darkness, God's people need to be lights; and when society is decaying because of sin, we need to be salt. We must be distinctive! Paul calls us to be "children of God without fault in a crooked and depraved generation" (Phil. 2:15). "If a man does not keep pace with his companions," wrote Henry David Thoreau in the conclusion to *Walden*, "perhaps it is because he hears a different drummer. Let him step to the music he hears, however measured or far away."

—*Warren W. Wiersbe*

How to Use This Study

This study is designed for both individual and small-group use. We've divided it into eight lessons—each references one or more chapters in Warren W. Wiersbe's commentary *Be Distinct* (second edition, David C Cook, 2010). While reading *Be Distinct* is not a prerequisite for going through this study, the additional insights and background Wiersbe offers can greatly enhance your study experience.

The **Getting Started** questions at the beginning of each lesson offer you an opportunity to record your first thoughts and reactions to the study text. This is an important step in the study process as those "first impressions" often include clues about what it is your heart is longing to discover.

The bulk of the study is found in the **Going Deeper** questions. These dive into the Bible text and, along with helpful excerpts from Wiersbe's commentary, help you examine not only the original context and meaning of the verses but also modern application.

Looking Inward narrows the focus down to your personal story. These intimate questions can be a bit uncomfortable at times, but don't shy away from honesty here. This is where you are asked to stand before the mirror of God's Word and look closely at what you see. It's the place to take a good look at yourself in light of the lesson and search for ways in which you can grow in faith.

Going Forward is the place where you can commit to paper those things you want or need to do in order to better live out the discoveries you made in the Looking Inward section. Don't skip or skim through this. Take the time to really consider what practical steps you might take to move closer to Christ. Then share your thoughts with a trusted friend who can act as an encourager and accountability partner.

Finally, there is a brief **Seeking Help** section to close the lesson. This is a reminder for you to invite God into your spiritual-growth process. If you choose to write out a prayer in this section, come back to it as you work through the lesson and continue to seek the Holy Spirit's guidance as you discover God's will for your life.

Tips for Small Groups

A small group is a dynamic thing. One week it might seem like a group of close-knit friends. The next it might seem more like a group of uncomfortable strangers. A small-group leader's role is to read these subtle changes and adjust the tone of the discussion accordingly.

Small groups need to be safe places for people to talk openly. It is through shared wrestling with difficult life issues that some of the greatest personal growth is discovered. But in order for the group to feel safe, participants need to know it's okay *not* to share sometimes. Always invite honest disclosure, but never force someone to speak if he or she isn't comfortable doing so. (A savvy leader will follow up later with a group member who isn't comfortable sharing in a group setting to see if a one-on-one discussion is more appropriate.)

Have volunteers take turns reading excerpts from Scripture or from the commentary. The more each person is involved, even in the mundane tasks, the more they'll feel comfortable opening up in more meaningful ways.

The leader should watch the clock and keep the discussion moving. Sometimes there may be more Going Deeper questions than your group can cover in your available time. If you've had a fruitful discussion, it's okay to move on without finishing everything. And if you think the group is getting bogged down on a question or has taken off on a tangent, you can simply say, "Let's go on to question 5." Be sure to save at least ten to fifteen minutes for the Going Forward questions.

Finally, soak your group meetings in prayer—before you begin, during as needed, and always at the end of your time together.

Parting Ways
(2 KINGS 1—2)

Before you begin ...
- *Pray for the Holy Spirit to reveal truth and wisdom as you go through this lesson.*
- *Read 2 Kings 1—2. This lesson references chapter 1 in* Be Distinct. *It will be helpful for you to have your Bible and a copy of the commentary available as you work through this lesson.*

Getting Started

From the Commentary

Elisha ("my God saves") had been Elijah's servant and apprentice for probably ten years, but now the time had come for the Lord to call home His courageous servant. We get the impression that they were men with different dispositions, Elijah being the "son of thunder" and Elisha the gracious healer. This doesn't mean that Elijah was never tender or that Elisha was never stern, for the biblical record shows otherwise. But in general, Elijah came like

John the Baptist, putting the ax to the root of the trees, while Elisha followed with a quiet ministry like that of Jesus (see Matt. 3:1–12; 11:16–19).

—*Be Distinct*, page 15

1. Why is it significant that Elijah's and Elisha's approaches to ministry were so different? What does this tell us about how God used His prophets in Old Testament times? What does it tell us about leaders in today's church?

2. Choose one verse or phrase from 2 Kings 1—2 that stands out to you. This could be something you're intrigued by, something that makes you uncomfortable, something that puzzles you, something that resonates with you, or just something you want to examine further. Write that here.

Going Deeper

From the Commentary

> After the death of wicked King Ahab, the nation of Moab took advantage of Ahaziah, his son and successor, and broke the bonds of vassalage that had chained them to Israel (2 Kings 1:1; see 3:4–5). Years before, David had defeated Moab (2 Sam. 8:2), and Ahaziah's successor, Jehoram (Joram), would join with Jehoshaphat, king of Judah, to fight against the Moabites (2 Kings 3:6ff.). But the Lord is in charge of the nations of the earth (Acts 17:24–28; Dan. 5:19, 21; 7:27), and His decrees determine history.
>
> —*Be Distinct*, pages 15–16

3. How does the Lord respond to a circumstance when He isn't allowed to rule? (See Ps. 33:10–11.) What are some of the ways God's decrees have determined history?

From the Commentary

> When Ahaziah was severely injured by falling through a lattice, he turned for guidance to Baal and not to the Lord God of Israel.

Why did the king decide to send messengers forty miles away to Ekron to consult the priests of Baal? True, Elijah had slain the 450 prophets of Baal (1 Kings 18:19–40), but that was ten years prior. Surely other priests of Baal were available in the land. The king's parents had fed hundreds of these priests at their table (1 Kings 18:19), and it wouldn't have been difficult for King Ahaziah to import priests of Baal to serve as court chaplains. Perhaps he sent to Ekron for help because he didn't want the people in Samaria to know how serious his condition was.

—*Be Distinct*, page 16

4. Why is it notable that Ahaziah asked the priests of Baal for a prognosis and not for healing? Why do you think he didn't ask Elijah? What impression of his relationship with Elijah do you get from 2 Kings 1:3–12?

More to Consider: "Baal" simply means "lord," and "Baal-Zebul" means "Baal is prince." But the devout remnant in Israel who worshipped Jehovah made changes in that name and ridiculed the false god of their neighbors. "Baal-Zebel" means "lord of the dung," and "Baal-Zebub" means "lord of the flies." Read Matthew 10:25 and note the context in which Jesus used a similar name. What does all of this teach us about the significance and importance of people's names in Bible history?

From Today's World

In Elijah's time, God's people struggled to know whom to follow—the Lord God, or one of the many pagan gods that defined the ancient cultures. While the prophets made it clear which was the way to turn, people who considered themselves "God's people" were often drawn away to other religions.

The church today is suffering from a bit of an identity crisis. While many churches see shrinking membership (often due to young people leaving in droves), some continue to grow and thrive. There are a lot of reasons for the shifting membership, including a change in demographics, the role of technology, pluralism, and the public perception of religion. But while church attendance is declining, there's a growing pool of people who consider themselves "spiritual" without attaching themselves to a particular congregation or, in some cases, even an orthodox belief system.

5. Why are churches seeing such a decline in being a regular part of people's lives? What are the exceptions? What are those churches doing right? Is it a cause for concern that people are finding their "churches" in places outside of traditional congregations? What are the risks of seeking spiritual guidance outside of a traditional church? What are the possible benefits?

From the Commentary

It seems incredible that the king's messengers didn't know who Elijah was and didn't learn his identity until they returned to the palace! Elijah was Ahab's enemy (1 Kings 21:20), and Ahaziah was Ahab's son, so certainly Ahaziah had said something to his courtiers about the prophet.

The announcement that he would die should have moved Ahaziah to repent of his sins and seek the Lord, but instead, he tried to lay hands on the prophet. (This reminds us of King Herod's seizure of John the Baptist; Matt. 14:1–12.) Ahaziah knew that Elijah was a formidable foe, so he sent a captain with fifty soldiers to bring him to the palace; but he underestimated the prophet's power.

—*Be Distinct*, page 17

6. Review 2 Kings 1:5–12. How was the description the messengers gave of Elijah similar to that of John the Baptist? (See Luke 1:17; Matt. 3:3; 11:7–10.) Did Ahaziah think he could nullify Elijah's prophecy? Explain. What does this tell us about Ahaziah's belief in his own power and influence? How is this similar to the way some leaders today try to bypass God's will in order to present different agendas?

From the Commentary

King Ahaziah died, but Elijah didn't die! He was taken up into heaven in a whirlwind, accompanied by fiery horses drawing a chariot of fire. Like Enoch of old, he walked with God and then suddenly went to be with God (Gen. 5:21–24; Heb. 11:5). Both men illustrate the catching away of the saints when Jesus returns (1 Thess. 4:13–18). But before Elijah left Elisha to carry on the work, he walked with his successor from Gilgal to beyond the Jordan, and what a walk that must have been! The Lord had at least three purposes in mind when He led these two servants to walk together.

(1) Taking advantage of the present.

(2) Preparing for the future.

(3) Reviewing the past.

—*Be Distinct*, pages 19–22

7. Review 2 Kings 2:1–6. How did God help prepare Elisha for his work during this walk with Elijah? What does this walk teach us about mentoring? What does it reveal about God's plans for leaders? How can we use this model of growing leaders in today's church?

From the Commentary

> Elijah is a good model for believers to imitate when it comes to the inevitability of one day leaving this earth, either through death or the rapture of the church. He didn't sit around and do nothing, but instead visited three of the prophetic schools and no doubt ministered to the students. He didn't say to his successor "I'm going to leave you" and thus dwell on the negative, but said "I'm going to Bethel—to Jericho—to the Jordan" and kept busy until the very moment the Lord called him. Even more, he didn't ask his successor to give him anything, because we can't take anything in our hands from earth to heaven (1 Tim. 6:7), but instead he offered to give Elisha a gift before the end came.
>
> —*Be Distinct*, page 25

8. What are some of the ways believers today can model Elijah's approach to the end of his life? What are some of the "gifts" today's leaders can give to those who follow?

From the Commentary

Elijah didn't give his successor three wishes; he simply asked him to name the one gift he wanted more than anything else. Every leader needs to be right in his priorities, and Elisha had a ready answer: He wanted a double portion of the spirit of his master.... The request was based on Deuteronomy 21:17, the law of inheritance for the firstborn. Though there were many "sons of the prophets," Elisha saw himself as Elijah's "firstborn son," who deserved the double inheritance that Moses commanded. Like a firstborn son serving a father, Elisha had walked with Elijah and attended to his needs (2 Kings 3:11; 1 Kings 19:21), but the only inheritance he desired was a double measure of his master's inner spirit of courage, faithfulness, faith in God, and obedience to God's will. In saying this, Elisha was accepting the prophetic ministry that Elijah had begun and declaring that he would carry it on to completion, with God's help.

Elijah was honest with his friend and told him that such a gift was not his to grant, for only the Lord could do it. However, if the Lord allowed Elisha to see his translation from earth to heaven, that would be proof that his request had been granted. Then it happened! As the two friends walked along talking, a fiery chariot drawn by fiery horses came between them, and a whirlwind lifted Elijah out of sight—*and Elisha saw it happen!* This meant his request had been granted and the Lord had equipped him to continue the ministry of Elijah.

—*Be Distinct*, pages 25–26

9. Why was Elisha's request not Elijah's to grant? Why would Elisha ask for such a gift? What does God's response to this request tell us about how He answers such prayers? What does it reveal about Elisha?

More to Consider: Why did Elijah leave the Promised Land and go to the other side of the Jordan? Certainly God's whirlwind could have lifted him just as easily from Bethel or Jericho. In what ways might this have been a lesson God used to teach Elisha more about trust?

From the Commentary

The event in 2 Kings 2:23–25 took place at Bethel, one of the centers for idol worship in the land (1 Kings 12:28–33; Amos 7:13). The Hebrew word translated "little children" in the KJV really means "youths" or "young men." It refers to people from twelve to thirty years old who were able to discern right from wrong and make their own decisions. This was not a group of playful children making a clever joke but a gang of smart-aleck youths maliciously ridiculing God and God's servant.

"Go up" refers to the recent ascension of Elijah to heaven. If the fifty men saw Elijah vanish from the earth in an instant, they certainly would have reported what had happened, and the event would have been discussed widely. The youths were saying, "If you are a man of God, why don't you get out of here and go to heaven the way Elijah did? We're glad he's gone and we wish you would follow him!" For a young person to call any grown man "bald head" would be a gross affront, and to repeat the nickname would make the offense even worse. Gray hair was a "crown of glory" (Prov. 16:31) among the Jews, but baldness was a rare thing among them and by some people was considered a disgrace (Isa. 3:24).

—*Be Distinct*, pages 29–30

10. Why did Elisha call down a curse on the mockers? What was the purpose of this response from God? In what ways was it a warning to the people?

Looking Inward

Take a moment to reflect on all that you've explored thus far in this study of 2 Kings 1—2. Review your notes and answers, and think about how each of these things matters in your life today.

Tips for Small Groups: To get the most out of this section, form pairs or trios and have group members take turns answering these questions. Be honest and as open as you can in this discussion, but most of all, be encouraging and supportive of others. Be sensitive to those who are going through particularly difficult times, and don't press for people to speak if they're uncomfortable doing so.

11. What is your ministry style? How is it similar to or different from those of your family members and friends? What are some ways your unique ministry style reaches people whom others can't?

12. Describe a time when you sought answers from a source other than the church or God's Word. What prompted that search? Why did you choose not to seek God's answer to the situation? What did you learn from that experience?

13. What sort of "gifts" would you want your pastors and leaders to grant you upon their departure? What do you most long for in your ministry to others?

Going Forward

14. Think of one or two things you have learned that you'd like to work on in the coming week. Remember that this is all about quality, not quantity. It's better to work on one specific area of life and do it well than to work on many and do poorly (or to be so overwhelmed that you simply don't try).

Do you want to learn how to best use your ministry style for God's work? Be specific. Go back through 2 Kings 1—2 and put a star next to the phrase or verse that is most encouraging to you. Consider memorizing that verse.

Real-Life Application Ideas: This week, take an Elijah walk with one of your most trusted leaders. During that time, invite him or her to share leadership and ministry wisdom with you. This is a time to soak up whatever you can so you can better serve God in your own unique role in ministry. Later, lead someone else on an Elijah walk of your own, offering your accumulated wisdom to a child or a person you're mentoring or someone else who is younger than you in the faith. Repeat these walks often and use the time to grow your relationship with God.

Seeking Help

15. Write a prayer below (or simply pray one in silence), inviting God to work on your mind and heart in those areas you've noted in the Going Forward section. Be honest about your desires and fears.

Notes for Small Groups:
- *Look for ways to put into practice the things you wrote in the Going Forward section. Talk with other group members about your ideas, and commit to being accountable to one another.*
- *During the coming week, ask the Holy Spirit to continue to reveal truth to you from what you've read and studied.*
- *Before you start the next lesson, read 2 Kings 3—4. For more in-depth lesson preparation, read chapter 2, "Amazing Grace," in* Be Distinct.

Grace
(2 KINGS 3—4)

Before you begin ...
- *Pray for the Holy Spirit to reveal truth and wisdom as you go through this lesson.*
- *Read 2 Kings 3—4. This lesson references chapter 2 in* Be Distinct. *It will be helpful for you to have your Bible and a copy of the commentary available as you work through this lesson.*

Getting Started

From the Commentary

From the outset of his ministry, Elisha proved himself to be a worker of miracles like his master and predecessor, Elijah, for he opened the Jordan River and crossed on dry land, and then he purified the water at Jericho. Except for calling down judgment on a group of arrogant young men (2 Kings 2:23–25), Elisha's miracles were primarily revelations of God's grace and mercy. Elijah reminds us of John the Baptist with his ax, winnowing fork, and baptism of fire (Matt. 3:1–12; Luke 1:17), but Elisha reminds us of our Savior, who had compassion on the multitudes and "went about doing good" (Acts 10:38).

—*Be Distinct*, page 35

1. How do the miracles recorded in 2 Kings 3—4 magnify the grace of God? Why is that important? How does God's grace play out differently in the Old Testament than in the New Testament?

2. Choose one verse or phrase from 2 Kings 3—4 that stands out to you. This could be something you're intrigued by, something that makes you uncomfortable, something that puzzles you, something that resonates with you, or just something you want to examine further. Write that here.

Going Deeper

From the Commentary

> When Ahaziah died, his brother Joram became king of
> Israel (2 Kings 1:17). He was also called Jehoram, but
> since that was also the name of Jehoshaphat's son and
> the coregent of Judah, we'll distinguish the two rulers
> by calling the king of Israel Joram. Being a son of Ahab
> and Jezebel, the new king was hardly a godly man, but at
> least he removed an image dedicated to Baal (constructed
> in 1 Kings 16:32–33), and he showed some respect for
> Elisha. However, neither Baal worship nor the golden
> calves were removed from the land during his reign, and
> the image of Baal that Joram removed found its way back
> and Jehu had to destroy it (2 Kings 10:27).
>
> —*Be Distinct*, pages 35–36

3. Review 2 Kings 3. Why might the otherwise ungodly king remove the
pagan image and show respect to the prophet Elisha? What did this say
about his leadership? About his beliefs? Did this make him a better leader
than one who might have decried all the Israelites' beliefs about the one
true God? Explain.

More to Consider: The land of Moab was especially suited for raising sheep, but an annual tribute to Israel of 100,000 lambs and the wool of 100,000 rams was certainly demanding. Ahab's death and Ahaziah's brief reign of less than two years gave Mesha, king of Moab, opportunity to rebel. When Joram, a younger man, took the throne of Israel, it seemed like an opportune time for Moab to break the yoke once and for all. Why did Joram respond to this threat by taking a military census and preparing for war? What message was he trying to present about his approach to leadership? Was he acting out of fear? Explain.

From the Commentary

Jehoram, now coregent of Judah, was married to Joram's sister Athaliah, so it seemed only right for Joram to ask King Jehoshaphat to go with him to punish Moab. A year before, the Moabites and Ammonites had declared war on Judah, and Jehoshaphat had soundly defeated them with the Lord's help (2 Chron. 20). Joram wanted allies like that at his side! The two kings decided not to attack from the north because the northern border of Moab was heavily fortified and the Ammonites might interfere, but to make an attack from around the southern extremity of the Dead Sea. Joram's army would march south through Judah and pick up Jehoshaphat's men, and then both armies would march through Edom and join with the Edomite army at the more vulnerable southern border of Moab.

The plan was a good one. Joram's army left Samaria and after a three-day march joined Jehoshaphat's army in Judah, probably at Jerusalem. Then both armies proceeded south to Edom, a journey of about four days. So, after this seven-day march, the armies arrived at the valley at the southern end of the Dead Sea, between the mountains of Judah and Moab. Everything was going well except that they were out of water. The soldiers were thirsty, and so were the baggage animals and the cattle brought along for food.

—*Be Distinct*, page 36

4. How did King Joram respond to the situation he found himself in? (See 2 Kings 3:10.) Why is this notable? What was Jehoshaphat's response? In what ways was Elisha the most valuable man in the combined armies of the three nations?

From Today's Church

Prophets such as Elijah and Elisha were the most important people in the kingdom during times of war. But today, God's leaders seem to be without the guidance of prophets, at least prophets similar to those in the time of the kings. Today's pastors and leaders rely on the wisdom from mentors and committees and the accumulated wisdom of thousands found in books and other resources. There is certainly no dearth of material available to pastors and leaders today to help them sort through complex or controversial issues. All one has to do is search the Internet and a whole bevy of "wisdom" shows up.

5. Without the direct guidance from prophets of old, how do today's leaders of churches and even nations know which way to turn? How do leaders today know what is the godly approach to a conflict? What opportunities do we have today that God's people didn't have in the time of the prophets? Why is that significant to how we lead today?

From the Commentary

From the great international conflict, Elisha returned to the concerns of the schools of the prophets, for a true spiritual leader has a concern for individuals. He followed the example of his mentor, Elijah, who had ministered to families (1 Kings 17:8–24). The fact that the woman in 2 Kings 4 was a widow and the mother of two sons shows that the sons of the prophets weren't a celibate monastic group. Elisha knew this particular man and that he had a reputation for godliness. His death would have ended whatever income he earned, and for a widow to raise two sons unaided would have been a difficult thing at that time. Even dedicated people training for ministry have their trials and difficulties.

According to Hebrew law, a creditor could take the debtor and his children as servants, but he was not to treat them like slaves (Ex. 21:1–11; Lev. 25:29–31; Deut. 15:1–11). It would be heartbreaking for this woman to lose her husband to death and her two sons to servitude.

—*Be Distinct*, page 40

6. Review 2 Kings 4:1–7, then read Deuteronomy 10:18 and Psalms 68:5 and 146:9. What do these verses tell us about why God sent Elisha to help the woman? Why did Elisha ask the woman to close the door? Why did God choose to help this particular woman's situation but not others'? Does this mean we serve a capricious God? Explain.

From the Commentary

Shunem was about twenty miles northwest of Abel-meholah, Elisha's hometown, and twenty-five miles or so beyond Shunem was Mount Carmel (see 2 Kings 4:25). The average traveler on foot could cover fifteen to twenty miles per day, so Shunem was the perfect halfway point for Elisha whenever he went to Mount Carmel to pray, meditate, and seek the Lord in a new way. Since Mount Carmel was a very special place because of Elijah's ministry, perhaps there was also a school of the prophets there.

The unnamed woman referenced in 2 Kings 4:8–10 was great in social standing and in wealth. But she was also great in perception, for she noticed that Elijah often passed that way on his ministry trips. She also discerned that he was a man of God, and she wanted to serve the Lord by serving His prophet. We get the impression that her husband lacked his wife's spiritual insight, but at least he didn't oppose her hospitality to the itinerant preacher. He permitted her to have a permanent "prophet's chamber" built on the roof of the house and to outfit it with a lamp, a table and chair, and a bed. It was large enough to walk around in (v. 35) and apparently offered room enough for Gehazi, Elisha's servant (v. 13). The woman also saw to it that the two men were fed.

—*Be Distinct*, pages 41–42

7. How is 2 Kings 4:8–10 a model for godly hospitality? Why is this often a neglected ministry in today's church? What does Hebrews 13:2 teach us about the importance of hospitality? (See also 1 Peter 4:9; 1 Tim. 3:2; Titus 1:8.)

From the Commentary

The prophet and his servant were resting in the room when Elisha expressed a desire to do something special for the woman because of her kindness to them, and he asked Gehazi to call her so he could discuss the matter with her. Elisha addressed his words to Gehazi, possibly because the woman held Elisha in such high regard that she didn't feel worthy to speak with him. But her reply was humble and brief: "I am content among my own people." She didn't want Elisha to intercede with the great God because she had no desire to be treated like a great person. She ministered to them because she wanted to serve the Lord.

After she left the prophet's chamber, Gehazi suggested that she might want a son. Her husband was older than she, so perhaps conception was impossible, but if God could do it for Abraham and Sarah, He could do it for them. It was likely that her husband would precede her in death, and without a family, she would be left alone.

—*Be Distinct*, page 42

8. How is the message given to this woman similar to the promise God gave Abraham and Sarah? (See Gen. 17:21; 18:14; 2 Kings 4:16.) In what ways is this story an example of God's grace?

More to Consider: Review 2 Kings 4:29–37. Once again the door was shut prior to a miracle (2 Kings 4:4; and see Luke 8:51). First, the prophet prayed, and then, following the example of Elijah (1 Kings 17:17–24), he stretched himself out over the corpse. He got up and walked in the room, no doubt praying and seeking God's power, and then he lay on the boy a second time. This time the boy came back to life. What was Elisha's response to this miracle? Why did God seem intent on keeping miracles behind closed doors in these stories? What does that say about the miracles themselves? About the role Elisha and the prophets played in the miracles? Do we keep today's miracles "behind closed doors"? Explain.

From the Commentary

> Elisha visited the sons of the prophets at Gilgal during
> the time of the famine (2 Kings 8:1), and he commanded
> Gehazi his servant to make a stew for the men. Vegetables
> were scarce, so some of the men went looking in the fields
> for herbs they could add to the stew. The student who
> came with a cloak filled with gourds wasn't knowledge-
> able about such matters but just brought whatever looked
> edible. In fact, nobody knew what these gourds were!
>
> What were the evidences that there was poison in the pot?
> The bitter taste of the stew was perhaps the first clue, and
> the men probably suffered stomach pains and nausea.
> There had been death in the water at Jericho (2 Kings
> 2:19–22), and now there was death in the pot at Gilgal.
> It had been introduced innocently by a well-meaning
> student, but it had to be removed.
>
> —*Be Distinct*, page 45

9. How did Elisha solve the problem of the poisoned stew? How did this
stew serve as a metaphor for what the Israelites had been enduring? What
is the "poison" in our "stew" today? How has God, in His ultimate grace,
removed the poison?

From the Commentary

In the northern kingdom of Israel, there was no official temple dedicated to Jehovah, and many of the faithful priests and Levites had left apostate Israel and moved to Judah (1 Kings 12:26–33; 2 Chron. 11:13–17). Since there was no sanctuary to which the people could bring their tithes and offerings (Lev. 2:14; 6:14–23; 23:9–17; Deut. 18:3–5), they brought them to the nearest school of the prophets, where they would be shared by people true to the Mosaic law. The firstfruit offerings of grain could be roasted heads of grain, fine flour baked into cakes, or even loaves of bread. All of this would be most welcome to the sons of the prophets, and certainly the Lord honored the people who refused to bow down to the golden calves at Dan and Bethel.

There were one hundred hungry men in the group, and though the gifts the man brought were honored by the Lord, they couldn't feed all of the men adequately.

—*Be Distinct*, page 46

10. Review 2 Kings 4:42–44. How does this situation parallel that of Christ and the disciples? (See Matt. 14:13–21; 15:29–38.) In what ways is Gehazi's question "How can I set this before a hundred men?" similar to Andrew's question about the five loaves and two fish? (See John 6:9.) What was Elisha's response to this crisis of not enough food? What can we learn from his approach to the crisis?

Looking Inward

Take a moment to reflect on all that you've explored thus far in this study of 2 Kings 3—4. Review your notes and answers, and think about how each of these things matters in your life today.

Tips for Small Groups: To get the most out of this section, form pairs or trios and have group members take turns answering these questions. Be honest and as open as you can in this discussion, but most of all, be encouraging and supportive of others. Be sensitive to those who are going through particularly difficult times, and don't press for people to speak if they're uncomfortable doing so.

11. Describe a time when your beliefs and those of your boss or leader conflicted. How did you deal with that conflict? Did you ever resolve the differences? Explain. How can God's grace help people sort through these kinds of disagreements?

12. What is your experience with the ministry of hospitality? Is this a gift you share? Is it a gift you've received from others? Why is hospitality such an important ministry?

13. Have you ever been witness to a miracle? If so, describe the experience. How do you know it was a miracle? In what ways did you grow closer to Christ because of the experience?

Going Forward

14. Think of one or two things you have learned that you'd like to work on in the coming week. Remember that this is all about quality, not quantity. It's better to work on one specific area of life and do it well than to work on many and do poorly (or to be so overwhelmed that you simply don't try).

Do you want to trust God to intervene in a "famine" in your life? Be specific. Go back through 2 Kings 3—4 and put a star next to the phrase or verse that is most encouraging to you. Consider memorizing that verse.

Real-Life Application Ideas: One of the lessons in 2 Kings 3—4 teaches us about the great ministry of hospitality. This week, look for practical ways to show hospitality toward others. Perhaps you can prepare meals for a family or offer housing to someone who is traveling through your community. Model God's grace by serving others without expecting anything in return.

Seeking Help

15. Write a prayer below (or simply pray one in silence), inviting God to work on your mind and heart in those areas you've noted in the Going Forward section. Be honest about your desires and fears.

Notes for Small Groups:

- *Look for ways to put into practice the things you wrote in the Going Forward section. Talk with other group members about your ideas, and commit to being accountable to one another.*

- *During the coming week, ask the Holy Spirit to continue to reveal truth to you from what you've read and studied.*

- *Before you start the next lesson, read 2 Kings 5—7. For more in-depth lesson preparation, read chapters 3 and 4, "Three Men—Three Miracles" and "The Battle Is the Lord's," in* Be Distinct.

Miracles and More
(2 KINGS 5—7)

Before you begin …
- *Pray for the Holy Spirit to reveal truth and wisdom as you go through this lesson.*
- *Read 2 Kings 5—7. This lesson references chapters 3 and 4 in* Be Distinct. *It will be helpful for you to have your Bible and a copy of the commentary available as you work through this lesson.*

Getting Started

From the Commentary

Elisha was a miracle-working prophet who ministered to all sorts of people who brought him all kinds of needs. In 2 Kings 5:1—6:7, we see Elisha healing a distinguished general, judging his own servant, and helping a lowly student get back to work. It may seem a long way from the lofty head of the army to a lost axhead, but both were important to God and to God's servant. Like our Lord when He ministered here on earth, Elisha had time for individuals, and he wasn't influenced by their social standing or their financial worth. "Casting all your care upon Him, for He cares for you" (1 Peter 5:7 NKJV).

—*Be Distinct*, page 51

1. In what ways is the theme of "ministry" important in 2 Kings 5:1—6:7? How did God give Naaman a new purpose in life? What did the student get back in addition to the lost axhead? What does this teach us about how God effects change in people's lives?

More to Consider: The prophet Elijah is named twenty-nine times in the New Testament while Elisha is named only once. "There were many in Israel with leprosy in the time of Elisha the prophet, yet not one of them was cleansed—only Naaman the Syrian" (Luke 4:27). What does this tell us about Elijah? What does it tell us about the importance of Naaman's story? Why single this one out to share about Elisha's ministry?

2. Choose one verse or phrase from 2 Kings 5—7 that stands out to you. This could be something you're intrigued by, something that makes you

uncomfortable, something that puzzles you, something that resonates with you, or just something you want to examine further. Write that here.

Going Deeper

From the Commentary

The king of Syria was Ben Hadad II, and as commander of the army, Naaman was the number two man in the nation. But with all his prestige, authority, and wealth, Naaman was a doomed man because under his uniform was the body of a leper. It appears from 2 Kings 5:11 that the infection was limited to one place, but leprosy has a tendency to spread, and if left unchecked, it ultimately kills.

Elisha knew that Naaman had to be humbled before he could be healed. Accustomed to the protocol of the palace, this esteemed leader expected to be recognized publicly and his lavish gifts accepted with exaggerated appreciation, because that's the way kings did things. But Elisha didn't even come out of his house to welcome the man! Instead, he sent a messenger (Gehazi?) instructing him to ride thirty-two miles to the Jordan River and immerse himself in it seven times. Then he would be cleansed of his leprosy.

Naaman had been seeking help, and now his search was ended.

—*Be Distinct*, pages 52, 54

3. Why was it significant that Naaman had leprosy rather than another affliction? (See Lev. 13.) How did this provide God with an opportunity to reveal His power and grace? What was Naaman's response to his healing?

From the Commentary

Like every new believer, Naaman still had a lot to learn. He had been saved and healed by trusting in God's grace, and now he had to grow in grace and faith and learn how to live to please the God who saved him. Instead of hurrying home to share the good news, Naaman returned to the house of Elisha to thank the Lord and His servant. (See Luke 17:11–19.) That meant traveling another thirty miles, but he must have rejoiced during the entire trip. It was natural for him to want to reward Elisha, but had the prophet accepted the gift, he would have taken the credit to himself and robbed God of glory. God saves us "to the praise of the glory of his grace" (Eph. 1:6, 12, 14). He also would have given Naaman, a new convert, the impression that his gifts had something to do with his salvation. Abraham had refused the gifts from the king of Sodom (Gen. 14:17–24), Daniel would refuse the king's offer (Dan. 5:17), and Peter and John would reject Simon's money (Acts 8:18–24).

—*Be Distinct*, page 56

4. Why did Elisha refuse Naaman's gifts? In what ways was Naaman's understanding of the God who healed him incomplete? How is this similar to the way new believers today attempt to understand and apply their faith? How did Elisha respond to Naaman's errors?

From the Commentary

While Naaman was seeking to live the truth and please the Lord, Elisha's servant was wallowing in deception and unholy desires. "Thou shalt not covet" is the last of the

Ten Commandments (Ex. 20:17), but when you break this one commandment, you tempt yourself to break the other nine.

Gehazi had been decaying in his spiritual life, and this was the climax. He had pushed away the woman whose son died (2 Kings 4:27), and he had no power to raise the boy to life (4:31). Now his covetousness took control, it led to lying, and it finally resulted in Gehazi becoming a leper.

—*Be Distinct*, pages 57–58

5. Why are we tempted to break the other commandments when we break "Thou shalt not covet"? How did Gehazi's leprosy typify the decay he was suffering on the inside? In what ways did he take the name of the Lord in vain? Why, ultimately, did he lose his ministry? How is this similar to what happens sometimes in today's church?

From the Commentary

New growth brings new obligations, and the education facilities at Jordan had to be enlarged. Schools today would do fund-raising and hire architects and contractors, but in Elisha's day, the students did the work. Not only that, but the leader of the school went with them and encouraged the work. Elisha had a shepherd's heart and was willing to go with his flock and share their burdens.

The Jewish people didn't have hardware stores stocked with tools such as we have today. Iron tools were precious and scarce, which explains why the student had to borrow an ax so he could help prepare the timber.

After the axhead slipped off its handle, the student was quick enough to see where it fell and honest enough to report the accident to Elisha. The Jordan isn't the cleanest river in the Holy Land (2 Kings 5:12), and it would be very difficult for anybody to see the axhead lying at the bottom. The prophet didn't "fish out" the axhead with a pole. He threw a stick into the water at the place where the axhead sank, and the Lord raised the iron axhead so that it floated on the surface of the river and could be picked up. It was a quiet miracle from a powerful God through a compassionate servant.

—*Be Distinct*, pages 61–62

6. Why did God decide to use a miracle to recover the axhead? What does the recovery of the axhead teach us about the value and importance of serving God? What does its recovery teach us about God Himself?

From the Commentary

> From our point of view, it would have been more logi-
> cal for the Lord to appoint Elijah, the "son of thunder,"
> to confront the enemy armies that invaded Israel, but
> instead, He appointed Elisha, the quiet farm boy. Elisha
> was like the "still, small voice" that followed the tumult of
> the wind, the earthquake, and the fire (1 Kings 19:11–12),
> just as Jesus followed John the Baptist, who had an ax
> in his hand. By declaring the righteousness of God and
> calling for repentance, Elijah and John the Baptist both
> prepared the way for their successors to minister, for with-
> out conviction there can be no true conversion.
>
> —*Be Distinct*, page 67

7. In what ways is God, not the prophet, the key actor in scriptural dramas? How did Elisha reveal God's character to God's people? In what ways was that dramatically different from the way the pagan idols worked?

From the Commentary

The young servant in 2 Kings 6:15–17 was an early riser, which speaks well of him, but he was still deficient in his faith. Seeing the city surrounded by enemy troops, he did the normal thing and turned to his master for help.

We wonder what promises from the Lord came to Elisha's mind and heart, for it's faith in God's Word that brings peace in the midst of the storm. Perhaps he recalled David's words in Psalm 27:3, "Though an army may encamp against me, my heart shall not fear; though war may rise against me, in this I will be confident" (NKJV). Or the words of Moses from Deuteronomy 20:3–4 may have come to mind, "Do not let your heart faint, do not be afraid ... for the LORD your God is He who goes with you, to fight for you against your enemies, to save you" (NKJV).

—*Be Distinct*, page 69

8. How did Elisha pray for the servant? In what ways was the servant living by sight and not by faith? In what ways does this situation parallel similar themes in the New Testament?

More to Consider: Elisha didn't ask the Lord to command the angelic army to destroy Ben Hadad's feeble troops. God gave Elisha a much better plan. Elisha had just prayed that the Lord would open his servant's eyes, but now he prayed that God would cloud the eyes of the Syrian soldiers. The soldiers' sight was altered in such a way that they were able to see but not comprehend. They were under the delusion that they were being led to the house of Elisha, but Elisha was leading them to the city of Samaria! Why did God choose this unique approach to solving the problem of the Syrian troops? What message was He sending His people through this action? What message does this give us today about how He works out His plan?

From the Commentary

Joram was appalled that the nation had fallen so low, and he publicly tore his robe, not as a sign of sorrow and repentance but as evidence of his anger at God and Elijah (see 2 Kings 5:7). When he did, he exposed the fact that he was wearing a rough sackcloth garment beneath the royal robe, but what good is sackcloth if there's no humility and repentance in the heart? His next words make it clear that he took no responsibility for the siege and the famine and that he wanted to murder Elisha. He even used the oath that he learned from his evil mother, Jezebel (6:31; 1 Kings 19:2). Joram's father, Ahab, called Elijah "the one who troubled Israel" (1 Kings 18:17), and Joram blamed Elisha for the plight Samaria was in at that time. The king sent a messenger to arrest Elisha and take him out to be killed.

—*Be Distinct*, page 73

9. Review 2 Kings 6:24—7:2. Whom did Joram blame for all the bad things happening in the kingdom? Why wasn't the prophet upset or worried about his fate? Elisha had already made it clear that he didn't accept the authority of the king of Israel because Joram was not of the line of David (2 Kings 3:14). How did this certainty inform the way he responded to Joram?

From the Commentary

How fortunate it was for the kingdom of Israel that they had Elisha the prophet living and ministering among them! Throughout Hebrew history, in times of crisis, the prophets had God's message for God's people, whether they obeyed it or not. King Joram could turn to the priests of Baal, but they had nothing to say. The Lord spoke through "his servants the prophets" (2 Kings 21:10).

Joram wanted something to happen now; he would wait no longer. But Elisha opened his message with "tomorrow about this time." What would happen? Food would once more be available, and the inflationary prices would fall drastically. The fine flour for the people and the barley for the animals would cost about twice as much as in normal times. This was a great relief from the prices the people had paid for unclean food.

The officer who attended the king didn't believe the words of the prophet and scoffed at what Elisha said. "Will it become like Noah's flood," he asked, "with food instead of rain pouring out of heaven?" (See Gen. 7:11. The Hebrew word translated "windows" in the KJV means "floodgates.")

—*Be Distinct*, page 74

10. Why was Joram so impatient? What did his impatience reveal about his heart? What detrimental role does impatience play in today's church? Where do believers turn to find the patience they need to wait on the Lord?

Looking Inward

Take a moment to reflect on all that you've explored thus far in this study of 2 Kings 5—7. Review your notes and answers, and think about how each of these things matters in your life today.

Tips for Small Groups: To get the most out of this section, form pairs or trios and have group members take turns answering these questions. Be honest and as open as you can in this discussion, but most of all, be encouraging and supportive of others. Be sensitive to those who are going through particularly difficult times, and don't press for people to speak if they're uncomfortable doing so.

11. What are some of the hard lessons about faith you've had to learn since you became a believer? How did you learn those truths? What does it mean to you to be constantly growing in your faith? How do you keep growing?

12. When do you most struggle with covetousness? How has this led to poor decisions? What is the best remedy for coveting? How can God's grace help you deal with moments when you feel a lack or a longing in life?

13. What are some ways you're impatient with God? How does He respond to your impatience? How does patience grow your faith?

Going Forward

14. Think of one or two things you have learned that you'd like to work on in the coming week. Remember that this is all about quality, not quantity. It's better to work on one specific area of life and do it well than to work on many and do poorly (or to be so overwhelmed that you simply don't try).

Do you want to become better at trusting God's timing? Be specific. Go back through 2 Kings 5—7 and put a star next to the phrase or verse that is most encouraging to you. Consider memorizing that verse.

Real-Life Application Ideas: One of the repeated themes in Elisha's story is that of listening to the still, small voice of God. This week, take extra time before your day begins, then also at mealtimes and at the end of the day, to sit in silence, simply listening to what God might have to say to you. Don't go into those quiet times with preconceived notions of what God might say—just invite the Holy Spirit to speak to you, then listen.

Seeking Help

15. Write a prayer below (or simply pray one in silence), inviting God to work on your mind and heart in those areas you've noted in the Going Forward section. Be honest about your desires and fears.

Notes for Small Groups:

- *Look for ways to put into practice the things you wrote in the Going Forward section. Talk with other group members about your ideas, and commit to being accountable to one another.*

- *During the coming week, ask the Holy Spirit to continue to reveal truth to you from what you've read and studied.*

- *Before you start the next lesson, read 2 Kings 8—11 and 2 Chronicles 21—23. For more in-depth lesson preparation, read chapters 5 and 6, "Reaping the Harvest of Sin" and "The Sword and the Crown," in* Be Distinct.

Sin

(2 KINGS 8—11; 2 CHRONICLES 21—23)

Before you begin ...

- *Pray for the Holy Spirit to reveal truth and wisdom as you go through this lesson.*
- *Read 2 Kings 8—11 and 2 Chronicles 21—23. This lesson references chapters 5 and 6 in* Be Distinct. *It will be helpful for you to have your Bible and a copy of the commentary available as you work through this lesson.*

Getting Started

From the Commentary

Eliphaz said some foolish things to his suffering friend Job, but he also stated some eternal principles, one of them being, "Even as I have seen, those who plow iniquity and sow trouble reap the same" (Job 4:8 NKJV). Solomon repeated this truth in Proverbs 22:8, "He who sows iniquity will reap sorrow" (NKJV), and the prophet Hosea put it graphically when he said, "They sow the wind, and reap the whirlwind" (Hos. 8:7 NKJV). Jeroboam, Omri, and Ahab had led the northern kingdom of Israel into idolatry; and Jehoram, who married a daughter of Ahab, had introduced Baal worship into the kingdom of Judah. Both kingdoms were rebellious against the Lord and polluted by idolatry, but now the day of judgment had arrived for Ahab's dynasty, the day that the prophet Elijah had predicted (1 Kings 21:21, 29).

—*Be Distinct*, page 81

1. Why is the theme of a day of judgment used so often in the Old Testament? What does this say about God's people during this time in history? How did all of this change with Jesus' life, death, and resurrection?

2. Choose one verse or phrase from 2 Kings 8—11 or 2 Chronicles 21—23 that stands out to you. This could be something you're intrigued by, something that makes you uncomfortable, something that puzzles you, something that resonates with you, or just something you want to examine further. Write that here.

Going Deeper

From the Commentary

> At the very moment Gehazi was describing the resurrection miracle, the mother of the child walked into the throne room! She had returned home only to discover that strangers had taken over her estate and robbed her of seven years' produce. In those days, it was common for people to bring such problems directly to the king and he would decide how property should be divided. The fact that Gehazi stood there as witness to her ownership of the land made it easy for the king to pass judgment. Years before, when her son had died, little did the mother realize that one day that bitter experience would play an important part in the preservation of her property.
>
> Our English word *providence* comes from two Latin words, *pro* and *video*, which together mean "to see ahead, to see before." God not only knows what lies ahead, but He plans what is to happen in the future and executes His plan perfectly.
>
> —*Be Distinct*, page 83

3. Review 2 Kings 8:5–6. In what ways does this episode reveal the character of God? What does it teach us about His providence? Does God's providence interfere with our power of choice? Explain. (See also 1 Chron. 29:11; Job 41:11; Pss. 95:3–5; 135:6; 139:13–18; Dan. 4:35; James 4:13–15.)

More to Consider: When the Lord met with Elijah on Mount Horeb, He gave the prophet a threefold commission: to anoint Hazael king of Syria, to anoint Jehu king of Israel, and to anoint Elisha to minister as Elijah's successor (1 Kings 19:8–18). Before his translation to heaven, Elijah had fulfilled only one of those commissions, the anointing of Elisha (vv. 19–21). How do the other commissions get fulfilled? What does this teach us about delegation? About our responsibility to fulfill God's plans?

From the Commentary

In 2 Kings 8:16–29 (and 2 Chronicles 21), the writer now shifts to the southern kingdom of Judah and tells us how King Jehoram brought apostasy and judgment to the land. For five years Jehoram served as coregent with his father, Jehoshaphat, and when Jehoshaphat died, he took the throne. Jehoram was married to Athaliah, a daughter of Ahab, and Jehoshaphat had joined Ahab in fighting against the Syrians at Ramoth Gilead (1 Kings 22). In other words, the wall of separation was gradually crumbling between David's dynasty in Judah and the descendants of Ahab in Israel.

—*Be Distinct*, page 86

4. How was Jehoram playing into the enemy's hands? In what ways did compromising with the evil rulers of Israel weaken his nation? How did God respond to Jehoram's failings as a ruler?

From the Commentary

In 2 Kings 9:1–13, the scene shifts to Ramoth Gilead, where Israel and Judah had combined their forces to recover the city from the Syrians. One of the key commanders of the Israeli army was Jehu, the son of Jehoshaphat, but not the Jehoshaphat who was king of Judah and the father of Jehoram. Unknown to Jehu, the prophet Elisha had dispatched one of the young sons of the prophets to anoint him king of Israel. This was the third assignment God gave Elijah (1 Kings 19:15–16). Instead of going to the battlefield himself, Elisha wisely gave the young man the authority to anoint Jehu privately. Elisha advised the student to flee the scene as fast as he could, for obviously there was going to be serious conflict.

Jehu was having a staff meeting in the courtyard when the young man approached and asked for a private audience with the commander. They went into a private room in the house and there the young man anointed Jehu to be the new king of Israel. It's interesting that the young prophet called the people of Israel "the people of the Lord" (2 Kings 9:6). Even though Israel and Judah were separate kingdoms and not obedient to the covenant, the people were still the chosen ones of the Lord and Abraham's descendants. God's covenants with Abraham (Gen. 12:1–3) and with David (2 Sam. 7) would still stand. The people had turned away from the Lord, but He had not forsaken them.

—*Be Distinct*, page 89

5. What was the main expectation put on Jehu as the anointed king of Israel? Why didn't he immediately announce that he was king? How did he fulfill the expectations given to him?

From the Commentary

It didn't take long for Jezebel and the palace residents to hear that Jehu was in Jezreel, that he was king, and that he had killed her son Joram. She put on her makeup, "attired her head," and watched at an upper window, waiting for him to show up. When she saw him come through the gate, she called, "Is it well, Zimri, your master's murderer?" (2 Kings 9:31 NASB). About fifty years before, Zimri had killed King Elah, made himself king, and then had proceeded to exterminate the family of Baasha (1 Kings 16:8–20). Since Zimri ruled for only seven days and then committed suicide, Jezebel was obviously trying to warn Jehu that his authority was weak and his days were numbered. She might even have been suggesting that Jehu form an alliance with her and strengthen his throne.

But Jehu knew his mandate from the Lord. When he called for evidence of loyalty from the palace personnel, two or three servants responded, and they threw Jezebel out the window to the courtyard below. Jehu rode his horse over her body until he was sure she was dead. Since he was now king, Jehu went into the palace and called for something to eat. As he was dining, he remembered that, evil as she was, Jezebel was a princess, the daughter of Ethbaal, the Sidonian ruler (1 Kings 16:29–31), so he ordered the servants to bury her body. But it was too late.

—*Be Distinct*, page 92

6. Jezebel's death is a vivid reminder of the dramatic way God responded to rebellion in Old Testament times. Why include this in the Bible? What does it teach us about God in Old Testament times? How does reading about this judgment and others like it help us better understand Jesus' role in our redemption?

From the Commentary

Studying 2 Kings 10 and 11 gives you the feeling that you're reading the morning paper or watching the ten o'clock news on television. You meet two leaders—Jehu, former army commander and now ruler of the northern kingdom of Israel, and Jehoiada, high priest at the temple in Jerusalem in the southern kingdom. As you watch these two men, you recognize the fact that the same forces for good and for evil were at work in their world that are at work in our own world today.

You also recognize the difference between leaders who are motivated by selfish ambition and leaders who are motivated by spiritual dedication. Jehu was proud of his "zeal for the LORD" (2 Kings 10:16), but that "zeal" was a pious cloak that hid the egotism and anger that really motivated his service. God gave Jehu an important work to do, but the king went beyond the assigned boundaries and carried his mandate too far. The Lord commended Jehu for what he accomplished (10:30), but He also chastened him for his pride and compromise.

—*Be Distinct*, page 97

7. How are Jehu's "pride and compromise" similar to what happens to some church leaders today? What are some of the ways a leader's zeal pushes him or her too far? What is our responsibility as believers in dealing with leadership that goes too far?

From the Commentary

> To prove that he intended to obey God and purge the
> land of Ahab's family, Jehu proceeded to kill all of Ahab's
> descendants that he found in Jezreel. But he didn't stop
> there; he went beyond his divine commission and killed
> Ahab's close friends, his chief officers, and the priests who
> served in the palace. It was a wholesale slaughter based on
> "guilt by association." The Lord wanted to rid the land
> of Ahab's family so that none of them could usurp the
> throne, but for Jehu to kill Ahab's friends, officers, and
> priests was totally unnecessary. In fact, Jehu later had seri-
> ous problems with the Syrians (2 Kings 10:22–23) and
> could have used some of the wisdom and experience of
> the court officers he killed. By wiping out these former
> leaders, Jehu destroyed a valuable source of political wis-
> dom and skill.
>
> —*Be Distinct*, page 101

8. Why did Jehu take things too far? What was the underlying motivation
for his actions? In what ways is this an example of how power can corrupt
someone? What kept Jehu from hearing God during this time?

More to Consider: Jehu encountered an ally, Jehonadab the Rechabite, and used him to give respectability to his own ambitions. The Rechabites were a people who belonged to the Kenites, the descendants of Moses' brother-in-law Hobab (Judg. 4:11). They identified with the tribe of Judah but stayed to themselves and followed the traditions laid down by their ancestors (Jer. 35). They were respected highly by the Jewish people, but being nomads and tent dwellers, the Rechabites were separated from the everyday city life and politics of the Jews. How did Jehu "use" Jehonadab to make his crusade look credible? What are other examples of this in history? Why do ambitious leaders seem to always choose a respectable second man to support their causes?

From the Commentary

Jehu had finished the work of ridding the nation of Ahab's family, so there were no descendants who could challenge his right to the throne. But what about the Baal worship that had infected the land? That was Jehu's next responsibility and he decided to use deception as his major weapon.

As king of Israel, Jehu could have dealt with the Baal worshippers in one of three ways. He could have commanded them to leave the land, or he could have obeyed Deuteronomy 13 and killed them. He might even have tried to convert them, although it would have been easy to "convert" if the sword was hanging over your head.

—*Be Distinct*, pages 102–3

9. What course of action did Jehu take? Why did he lie to the people first? Why did he pretend to be devoted to Baal? Or was he really pretending? How might the people under his rule have received his act of blatant deception?

From the Commentary

When God began to restore true worship in Jerusalem and Judah, He started with one dedicated couple—Jehoiada the high priest and his wife, Jehosheba. They enlisted the nurse who cared for Joash, and God protected all four of them for six years. Then Jehoiada enlisted the five military captains, who in turn assembled their five hundred soldiers. The scattered priests, Levites, and people of the land came together as one to honor the Lord and obey His Word. Sin was purged, God's will was accomplished, and the name of the Lord was glorified!

—*Be Distinct*, page 111

10. What does the story of Jehoiada and Jehosheba teach us about how God uses people to change the world? How did they lead the way to accomplishing God's will? How does God do the same thing even today?

Looking Inward

Take a moment to reflect on all that you've explored thus far in this study of 2 Kings 8—11 and 2 Chronicles 21—23. Review your notes and answers, and think about how each of these things matters in your life today.

> *Tips for Small Groups: To get the most out of this section, form pairs or trios and have group members take turns answering these questions. Be honest and as open as you can in this discussion, but most of all, be encouraging and supportive of others. Be sensitive to those who are going through particularly difficult times, and don't press for people to speak if they're uncomfortable doing so.*

11. Have you ever experienced God's providence? Explain. What difference does it make to you that God orchestrates events in order to make His will known? How does your personal choice play into God's orchestrations?

12. Have you ever lied or deceived someone in order to accomplish something for God? Explain. What prompted you to choose deception as a method for accomplishing this goal? Was there another way? If so, why didn't you choose that option? Is lying ever an appropriate way to follow God or do God's will? Why or why not?

13. What are some ways God is using you to accomplish His will? What are some obstacles that make it difficult for you to do God's will? How do you address those obstacles?

Going Forward

14. Think of one or two things you have learned that you'd like to work on in the coming week. Remember that this is all about quality, not quantity. It's better to work on one specific area of life and do it well than to work on many and do poorly (or to be so overwhelmed that you simply don't try).

Do you want to look over your life for signs of God's providence? Be specific. Go back through 2 Kings 8—11 and 2 Chronicles 21—23 and put a star next to the phrase or verse that is most encouraging to you. Consider memorizing that verse.

Real-Life Application Ideas: One of the themes in this section of 2 Kings is selfish ambition. This week, pay careful attention to the motivations behind your actions. Check yourself at work—are you making decisions in order to make yourself look better, or are you making the best decisions? Are you more concerned about being right than doing the right thing? Look at all the areas in which you have influence over others, and adjust your attitude to one of humility where necessary.

Seeking Help

15. Write a prayer below (or simply pray one in silence), inviting God to work on your mind and heart in those areas you've noted in the Going Forward section. Be honest about your desires and fears.

Notes for Small Groups:

- *Look for ways to put into practice the things you wrote in the Going Forward section. Talk with other group members about your ideas, and commit to being accountable to one another.*

- *During the coming week, ask the Holy Spirit to continue to reveal truth to you from what you've read and studied.*

- *Before you start the next lesson, read 2 Kings 12—13 and 2 Chronicles 24. For more in-depth lesson preparation, read chapter 7, "Focusing on Faith," in* Be Distinct.

Faith
(2 KINGS 12—13; 2 CHRONICLES 24)

Before you begin ...
- *Pray for the Holy Spirit to reveal truth and wisdom as you go through this lesson.*
- *Read 2 Kings 12—13 and 2 Chronicles 24. This lesson references chapter 7 in* Be Distinct. *It will be helpful for you to have your Bible and a copy of the commentary available as you work through this lesson.*

Getting Started

From the Commentary

It's a well-known principle that what a person believes ultimately determines how a person behaves. Eve believed the Devil's lie that she wouldn't die; she ate the forbidden fruit, and she eventually died. With his eyes wide open, Adam believed he should imitate his wife, so he took the fruit and ate it, and he plunged the human race into sin and death (Gen. 3; Rom. 5:12–21; 1 Tim. 2:14). When we believe the truth, God works for us, but when we believe a lie, the Devil works against us. When our Lord was tempted by Satan, He countered Satan's lies with God's truth and said, "It is written" (Matt. 4:1–11). The three kings presented in 2 Kings 12—13 illustrate three different kinds of faith, none of which is the kind God's people should have today.

—*Be Distinct*, page 115

1. Why is faith the most important piece of a believer's story? What are the kinds of faith described in 2 Kings 12—13 and 2 Chronicles 24? Why aren't they good examples of faith?

2. Choose one verse or phrase from 2 Kings 12—13 or 2 Chronicles 24 that stands out to you. This could be something you're intrigued by, something that makes you uncomfortable, something that puzzles you, something that resonates with you, or just something you want to examine further. Write that here.

Going Deeper

From the Commentary

In His parable about the sower (Matt. 13:1–9, 18–23), Jesus explained that, from a spiritual viewpoint, there are four kinds of hearts, and they respond to the seed of the Word in four different ways. When the hard-hearted hear the Word, the seed can't get in, so Satan snatches it away. Shallow-hearted people receive the Word but provide no room for it to take root, so the shoots grow up but don't last. A plant can't grow and bear fruit if it doesn't have roots. Those with crowded hearts receive the seed, but the shoots are smothered by the weeds that should have been pulled up. The person with the heart that bears fruit is honest, repentant, understands the Word, and embraces it by faith. When it came to his own personal faith, King Joash had a shallow heart.

—*Be Distinct*, pages 115–16

3. Review 2 Kings 12 and 2 Chronicles 24:1–17. What are the clues that Joash had a shallow heart? In what ways was he disobedient to God? In what areas did he struggle?

More to Consider: Joash became king at seven years old. What does this suggest about his early reign? How would Jehoiada have influenced his early choices? How did Joash change once Jehoiada died?

From the Commentary

It isn't easy to mentor a young king and know just when to loosen and lengthen the restraining cords. Parents know this from raising their children to adulthood. Perhaps Jehoiada was taking charge too much and not gradually handing responsibility over to Joash. On the other hand, perhaps Jehoiada held the reins longer because he saw some weaknesses in the king's character and wanted to give him time to correct them. Maybe it was just a "generational problem." Whatever the cause, the king decided it was time to be set free from the rule of the Jewish priesthood and to begin to assert his authority. He chose the repairing of the temple as his focal point for freedom.

—*Be Distinct*, page 117

4. Why did Joash choose repairing the temple as his focal point? How would a building project such as this have affected the way others saw him as a leader? Why did the priests hesitate to support his plan?

From Today's Church

Building projects have been divisive throughout church history. Whether it's repainting the children's classrooms or buying land and putting up a whole new structure, any change that affects a church's budget is prime fodder for disagreement and dissension. More than a few churches have split over building projects. "We don't need this" butts heads with "This is how we grow" time and time again, and it is often only by God's grace that a congregation finds agreement and either completes the building project or cancels it.

5. What are the biggest challenges a church faces when considering a possible improvement project? What are some red flags that a project might not be in the church's best interest? What are some clues that a project might be exactly what the church needs to grow and thrive?

From the Commentary

Jehoiada prepared a large offering box, placed it in the temple by an entrance near the altar, and encouraged the people to bring their offerings for the repair of the temple. Of course, there were temple guards who kept their eyes on the box. When the people found out that the project was now under royal supervision and in the hands of the laity, this encouraged them to give even more. They knew that every gift they brought and placed in the box would go directly into the building project and not be diverted into other ministries, so they gave generously. King Josiah followed a similar plan when he repaired the temple nearly two hundred years later (2 Kings 22:1–7).

—*Be Distinct*, page 118

6. How was this financing plan received by the people? How does this compare to the way churches fund building programs today? What did the people's generosity say about their trust in Jehoiada and Joash? What is a good way for leaders today to establish trust with their congregations when a building project is underway?

From the Commentary

Jehoiada died at the advanced age of one hundred thirty. He was so beloved by the people that he was buried with the kings (2 Chron. 24:15–16). But when Jehoiada passed off the scene, King Joash showed his true colors and abandoned the faith. His apostasy wasn't the fault of Jehoiada, for the high priest had faithfully taught Joash the Scriptures. The problem was Joash's shallow faith and his desire to please the leaders of the land, "the officials of Judah" who visited Joash and asked him to be more lenient in matters of religion (vv. 17–18). He relented, and once again idolatry moved into Judah and Jerusalem.

Joash's apostasy was a sin of willful rebellion against God, for the king knew what the law of Moses taught about idolatry. But it was also a sin of ingratitude for all that Jehoiada had done for him. *Jehoiada and his wife had saved the king's life!* The high priest had taught him the truth of God's Word and had stood at Joash's side as he learned how to govern the people. But the king had never taken the truth into his heart and allowed it to take root.

Joash is a warning to us today. It isn't enough simply to know God's truth; we must obey His truth "from the heart" (Eph. 6:6).

—*Be Distinct*, page 120

7. Review 2 Chronicles 24:15–27. In what ways is Joash's story a warning to us today? How does his story speak to the importance of a person's character?

From the Commentary

> In 2 Kings 13:1–9, the focus moves from Judah to Israel
> and the reign of Jehu's son Jehoahaz. It's no surprise that
> he chose Jeroboam as his model, because his father had
> done the same thing (10:29). Jehoahaz would rather wor-
> ship the golden calves than the living God, but when he
> found himself in trouble, he turned to the Lord for help.
>
> The people of Israel shouldn't have been surprised when
> the Lord brought the Syrians against them, because the
> people knew the terms of the covenant God had made
> with them before they entered the land of Canaan. If
> they obeyed Him, He would give them victory over their
> enemies, but if they disobeyed, He would cause them to
> fall before their enemies (Lev. 26:17, 25, 33, 36–39; Deut.
> 28:25–26, 49–52).
>
> —*Be Distinct*, page 122

8. What were the consequences of Israel's sin? What was God's response
to Jehoahaz's plea? Did God's promised blessing of the people change the
king? Why or why not?

More to Consider: How many times can we call on the Lord when we're in trouble and then ignore Him when we're safe? Read Proverbs 1:24–33 and Isaiah 55:6–7. What do these passages reveal to us about relying on "crisis faith"?

From the Commentary

> We haven't heard from or about Elisha since 2 Kings 9:1, when he sent one of the sons of the prophets to anoint Jehu to be king of Israel. This means over forty years of silence as far as the record is concerned, yet Elisha was at work in the land and the Lord was with him. Now he was an old man and about to die, and the king of Israel went to see him. Let's at least give Jehoash credit for visiting the prophet and seeking his help. Was it Elisha who told Jehoahaz that God would send a deliverer (13:4–5)? Was his son Jehoash that deliverer? Only Elisha knew God's plan, and the king was wise enough to visit him.
>
> —*Be Distinct*, page 124

9. Why are spiritual leaders often unappreciated during their lifetimes? How did Elisha, even from his deathbed, continue to serve the Lord and His people? What does his example teach us about the value of "senior servants" in our churches?

From the Commentary

King Jehoash was not a man of faith, but he could follow directions. However, he lacked the spiritual discernment and insight that people have who live in the Word and walk by faith. When the prophet put his hands on the king's hands, it obviously symbolized a conveying of power from God. When Elisha commanded him to shoot an arrow toward the area where the Syrians were in control, it clearly spoke of victory over the enemy (Deut. 32:42; Ps. 120:4). This much the king could have understood because Elisha gave him a clear promise of victory.

But when Elisha told him to take the remaining arrows and strike the ground with them, he didn't have the spiritual understanding he needed to make the most of it. Had he been a faithful worshipper of the living God, he would have seen the truth, but he was blind like the dead idols he worshipped (Ps. 115:3–8). Shooting one arrow guaranteed victory, but the number of times he smote the ground determined how many victories God would give him. Because Jehoash had ignorant faith, he limited himself to only three victories over the Syrians.

—Be Distinct, page 125

10. How did Elisha respond to the king's ignorance and unbelief? Why is it important for us to not only know God's will but also understand it? (See Eph. 5:17; Ps. 103:7.) In what ways do the commandments and acts

of God reveal to us the character of God? Why is it so important for us to recognize God's character?

Looking Inward

Take a moment to reflect on all that you've explored thus far in this study of 2 Kings 12—13 and 2 Chronicles 24. Review your notes and answers, and think about how each of these things matters in your life today.

> *Tips for Small Groups: To get the most out of this section, form pairs or trios and have group members take turns answering these questions. Be honest and as open as you can in this discussion, but most of all, be encouraging and supportive of others. Be sensitive to those who are going through particularly difficult times, and don't press for people to speak if they're uncomfortable doing so.*

11. What does faith mean to you? How do you know if your faith is strong or shallow? What are some steps you can take to deepen your faith?

12. How do you build strong character? What are some ways you intentionally work on improving your character? What are the obstacles in maintaining a consistent character at home, at work, at church, and in your community?

13. Have you had a season of life when you've employed a "crisis faith"—a faith that shows up only when things are tough? Describe that season. Why is it harder to exercise your faith when things are good?

Going Forward

14. Think of one or two things you have learned that you'd like to work on in the coming week. Remember that this is all about quality, not quantity. It's better to work on one specific area of life and do it well than to work on many and do poorly (or to be so overwhelmed that you simply don't try).

Do you want to take a step toward a more consistent faith? Be specific. Go back through 2 Kings 12—13 and 2 Chronicles 24 and put a star next to the phrase or verse that is most encouraging to you. Consider memorizing that verse.

Real-Life Application Ideas: This week, honor in some way the "senior servants" in your life. These could be church members or family members or just the wise old man down the street. Do something specific and supportive for each of these servants. Perhaps that means taking someone out to lunch, or maybe it means sitting with some of them to listen and learn. Make this week all about celebrating the wisdom that has gone before you. And don't forget to keep your ears open for new understanding of God's will for your own life!

Seeking Help

15. Write a prayer below (or simply pray one in silence), inviting God to work on your mind and heart in those areas you've noted in the Going Forward section. Be honest about your desires and fears.

Notes for Small Groups:

- *Look for ways to put into practice the things you wrote in the Going Forward section. Talk with other group members about your ideas, and commit to being accountable to one another.*

- *During the coming week, ask the Holy Spirit to continue to reveal truth to you from what you've read and studied.*

- *Before you start the next lesson, read 2 Kings 14—17 and 2 Chronicles 25—28. For more in-depth lesson preparation, read chapters 8 and 9, "Nine Kings— Five Assassinations" and "A Tale of Two Kingdoms," in* Be Distinct.

Kings and Kingdoms

(2 KINGS 14—17; 2 CHRONICLES 25—28)

Before you begin ...
- *Pray for the Holy Spirit to reveal truth and wisdom as you go through this lesson.*
- *Read 2 Kings 14—17 and 2 Chronicles 25—28. This lesson references chapters 8 and 9 in* Be Distinct. *It will be helpful for you to have your Bible and a copy of the commentary available as you work through this lesson.*

Getting Started

From the Commentary

The history recorded in 2 Kings 14—15 and 2 Chronicles 25—27 reeks of selfish intrigue, bloodshed, moral decay, and repeated rebellion against the law of the Lord. Ancient Israel wasn't much different from society today. Not one king of Israel encouraged his people to repent and seek the Lord, and in Judah, Amaziah and Uzziah both committed acts of arrogant ambition that brought judgment from God. When Jeroboam II became king of

Israel in 782 BC, little did the people realize that in sixty years, the kingdom would be no more. As we look at these nine rulers, we can gain some practical insights into the will and ways of God as well as the terrible wages of sin.

—*Be Distinct*, page 131

1. What does this period of history reveal about the nature of humankind? About the struggles of God's people? Why does the Bible record the stories of both good leaders and bad leaders? What can the modern church learn from these stories?

2. Choose one verse or phrase from 2 Kings 14—17 or 2 Chronicles 25—28 that stands out to you. This could be something you're intrigued by, something that makes you uncomfortable, something that puzzles you, something that resonates with you, or just something you want to examine further. Write that here.

Going Deeper

From the Commentary

> Amaziah was the ninth king of Judah and the son of Joash
> (Jehoash), the "boy king," who in his later years turned
> away from the Lord, killed God's prophet, and was him-
> self assassinated (2 Chron. 24:15–26). Amaziah made an
> excellent beginning, but he later abandoned the Lord and
> was also assassinated (2 Kings 14:17–20). He saw to it that
> the men were executed who had killed his father, and he
> obeyed Deuteronomy 24:16 by judging only the offenders
> and not their families. Had he continued to obey God's
> Word, his life and reign would have been much different.
>
> —*Be Distinct*, pages 131–32

3. Consider some of Amaziah's sins: unbelief (2 Chron. 25:5–13); idolatry
(vv. 14–16); and pride (vv. 17–24). How did these particular sins play out
in his story? How do they plague the church today?

More to Consider: Rejecting a second warning from the Lord, Amaziah invaded Israel, where his army was soundly defeated. He was taken captive, going from palace to prison. The army of Israel invaded Judah and destroyed six hundred feet of the wall of Jerusalem, leaving the city vulnerable to future attacks. They also plundered treasures from the palace and from the temple of the Lord, and they even took some of the leaders as hostages. King Amaziah was in exile in Samaria for fifteen years (2 Kings 14:17) and then returned to Jerusalem briefly as coregent with his son (2 Chron. 26:1, 3). Why would such a leader be allowed to colead the nation after such a rocky start? What did this say about the people? What prompted him to flee to Lachish? What was his final legacy there? (See 2 Kings 14:18–20; 2 Chron. 25:27.)

From the Commentary

In 2 Kings 14:23–29, the record turns from Judah to Israel and to Jeroboam II, who had the longest reign of any of Israel's kings, forty-one years. He was not a good king when it came to spiritual matters, but he brought prosperity to the nation and delivered it from its enemies. Even back in those ancient days, the average citizen didn't care about the character of the nation's leaders so long as the people had food on their tables, money in their purses, and no fear of being invaded by their enemies.

Thanks to Assyria's victories over Syria, both Israel and Judah were finally relieved of the bondage of that persistent enemy, and both had opportunity to use their wealth and manpower for building instead of battling.... The kingdom of Israel reached the dimensions achieved in the days of Solomon (2 Kings 14:25, 28; 1 Kings 8:65). The Lord permitted these victories, not because the people or their king deserved them, but because He had pity on His people who were suffering under the rule of Syria (2 Kings 14:26; see Ex. 2:23–25).

The prosperity of Israel was only a veneer that covered sins and crimes that were an abomination in the sight of the Lord. The prophets Amos (1:1) and Hosea (1:1) ministered during Jeroboam's reign and warned that judgment was coming. Judgment did come in 722 BC, when the Assyrians invaded Israel.

What were the sins of this prosperous kingdom? For one thing, the rich were getting richer at the expense of the poor, who were exploited and abused.

—*Be Distinct*, pages 135–36

4. How can prosperity be a smoke screen for what's really going on with a nation? A company? A church? Even a family? What are the typical sins of a prosperous kingdom? How do the poor fare in such a situation? What would be a godly approach to prosperity?

From the Commentary

His given name was Azariah, which means "Jehovah has helped," but when he became king of Judah at age sixteen, he took the "throne name" Uzziah, which means "Jehovah is strength." The people made him king when his father, Azariah, was taken to Samaria after his foolish war against Jehoash, king of Israel (2 Kings 14:13).

During his father's fifteen years of captivity in Samaria, Uzziah ruled Judah and sought to do the will of God. After his father's death, Uzziah continued on the throne until he foolishly attempted to become a priest and God judged him by making him a leper. At that time, his son Jotham became coregent with his father. The record declares that Uzziah was king of Judah fifty-two years (2 Chron. 26:3), including his coregencies with his father, Azariah (fifteen years), and also with his son Jotham (possibly ten years).

From the very beginning of his reign, Uzziah showed himself to be a faithful worshipper of Jehovah, even though he didn't try to eliminate the "high places," the hill shrines where the Jewish people worshipped. They were supposed to go to the temple with their gifts and sacrifices for the Lord, but it was more convenient to visit a local shrine. Some of the high places were still devoted to pagan deities, such as Baal (2 Chron. 27:2), and it wasn't until the reigns of Hezekiah and Josiah that the high places were removed (2 Chron. 31:1; 2 Kings 23).

—*Be Distinct*, pages 137–38

5. Review 2 Kings 14:22 and 2 Chronicles 26:2–15. What were some of Uzziah's accomplishments? What does 2 Chronicles 26:5 reveal about those accomplishments? Uzziah had Zechariah as his counselor. What does this tell us about the importance of wise counsel? How do we assure that in our churches today?

From the Commentary

From Jeroboam I, the first king of Israel, to Hoshea, the last king of Israel, not one king is called "good." However, the kingdom of Judah didn't fare much better, for out of twenty kings who ruled after the kingdom divided, only eight of them could be called "good." In 2 Kings 15:8–31, we meet with five kings of Israel who were notorious for their godless character and evil deeds. Four of them were assassinated! Shallum reigned only one month, Zechariah six months, and Pekahiah for two years. Menahem, the cruelest of them all, reigned for ten years, and Pekah for twenty years. As the northern kingdom stumbled toward destruction, their rulers hastened the coming of the judgment of God.

—*Be Distinct*, page 141

6. Review 2 Kings 15:8–31. Why were there so many bad kings in Israel and Judah? What does this reveal about God's people during this time in history? What does it tell us about God's character?

From the Commentary

Jotham, son of Uzziah, began to reign when he was twenty-five years old and ruled for sixteen years (2 Chron. 27:1). He was coregent with his father after Uzziah was smitten with leprosy for invading the temple precincts. Jotham would be considered a good king, although his son Ahaz was a bad king. In fact, from Jotham, the eleventh king of Judah, to Zedekiah, the twentieth and last king of Judah, only Jotham, Hezekiah, and Josiah could be called good kings. That's three kings out of ten. The Lord kept David's lamp burning in Jerusalem all those years, but there came a time when He had to bring in the nation of Babylon and punish His people for their sins.

Like his father, Uzziah, Jotham was both a builder and a warrior. He repaired the walls of Jerusalem and the Upper Gate of the temple. He also built cities in the Judean mountains and fortresses and towers in the wooded areas. His army confronted the armies of Israel and Syria, and he won a great victory over the Ammonites and put them under a very heavy annual tribute—nearly four tons of silver and 62,000 bushels each of wheat and barley (2 Chron. 27:5). "So Jotham became mighty, because he prepared his ways before the LORD his God" (27:6 NKJV). We wonder how much more good he would have accomplished had he lived longer.

—*Be Distinct*, pages 143–44

7. In Hebrew history we frequently find a godly father begetting an ungodly son and an ungodly father begetting a godly son. What does this reveal about the human condition? How did Ezekiel deal with this interesting phenomenon in chapter 18 of his prophecy? Why was God longsuffering toward His people during those difficult and evil days? How did the promise of the Davidic line play into this not-so-pretty slice of biblical history?

From the Commentary

Ahaz was the son of Jotham, a good king, and the father of Hezekiah, a very good king, but he himself was not a godly man or even a good man. Instead of discovering and doing the will of God, Ahaz imitated the wicked kings of

Israel and even the pagan practices of Assyria. He even adopted the horrible worship practices of the pagans and sacrificed his son (2 Chron. 28:3 says "children," plural) to a pagan god, Baal or Molech, a practice that was clearly prohibited in the law of Moses (Lev. 18:21; Deut. 18:10). Each Jewish son was to be redeemed by a sacrifice and therefore belonged to the Lord (Ex. 13; Num. 18:14–16). How could a son who belonged to God be sacrificed to an idol? But Ahaz was a compromiser both in his religious practices and his political leadership.

—*Be Distinct*, pages 147–48

8. Review 2 Kings 16:5–9 and 2 Chronicles 28:5–21. What was Ahaz's political compromise? What are the dangers of compromising on religious and political issues? How can compromise reveal the true nature of a person?

More to Consider: When Ahaz died, he was buried in Jerusalem but not in the royal tombs (2 Kings 16:19–20; 2 Chron. 28:26–27). In this, he joined Jehoram (2 Chron. 21:20), Joash (24:25), and Uzziah (26:23), and Manasseh would join them (33:20). Why would a king's burial place have been significant to the people? What message was being sent every time a king wasn't buried in the royal tombs?

From the Commentary

Hoshea was the last ruler of the northern kingdom of Israel, for in his day (722 BC), the Assyrians invaded the land, deported many of the citizens, and repopulated Israel with Gentile peoples from lands Assyria had conquered. The kingdom of Israel became Samaria, named after the capital city, and it was a nation whose citizens were not pure Jews but a comingling of many ethnic strains.

God had given His people so many blessings, and now those blessings would fall into the hands of Assyria and Babylon. The Jews had a living Lord, but they replaced Him with dead idols. Their wealthy land was confiscated by enemy nations, the people were taken captive, and eventually Jerusalem and the temple were destroyed (586 BC). God in His mercy preserved a faithful remnant so a light would remain shining and He could fulfill the promises He had made to His people.

—*Be Distinct*, page 153

9. Why did the Jews keep forsaking God? What was the ultimate result of their disobedience? What made it so hard for them to learn from their past ways? How is this similar to the way believers today struggle with changing patterns of sinful behavior? What advantages do believers have today that the Jews didn't have in the time of the kings?

From the Commentary

It's often been said that the one thing we learn from history is that we don't learn from history. In spite of the way the Lord had warned them and chastened them, the people continued to worship the Lord along with the other gods, and they did it their own way. They ignored their history as the people of God delivered from Egyptian bondage. They forgot God's laws and covenants, especially God's commandments concerning idolatry (Ex. 20:1–6). Like many professed Christians today, the people of Israel worshipped the Lord where and how they pleased, but they also paid respect to the false gods of the other nations.

What finally happened to these ten disobedient tribes? We hear about "the ten lost tribes of Israel," but the Bible never uses that phrase. Many people in the ten tribes assimilated with the peoples brought into the land by the Assyrians, and this produced the Samaritan people. But there's no evidence in Scripture that the ten tribes of Israel are "lost." Long before the Assyrians captured the northern kingdom, dedicated people from the ten tribes moved to Judah and remained faithful to the Lord (1 Kings 12:16–20; 2 Chron. 11:5–16; 19:4–10). Godly King Hezekiah invited true believers to come to Judah and worship God according to the Scriptures, and many of them came (2 Chron. 30:1–14, 25–27). Josiah's reforms had a tremendous effect on the Jewish people (2 Chron. 34:1–7, 33; 35:17–19).

Though Jesus spoke about "the lost sheep of the house of Israel" (Matt. 10:5–6), the New Testament knows nothing about any "lost tribes of Israel." (See Matt. 4:12–16; Luke 2:36–38.) Paul spoke about "our twelve tribes" (Acts 26:7), and James wrote his epistle "to the twelve tribes scattered abroad" (James 1:1). If we take Revelation 7:1–8 literally, then in the last days the Lord will find people from the tribes of Israel.

—Be Distinct, pages 156–57

10. What is the main message from 2 Kings 17? How does false worship lead to corrupt practices? How did the succession of (mostly) bad leaders make it inevitable that the people would lose their kingdom? Are there any parallels to this downfall in today's world? Explain. What is the solution to stopping a downward spiral of disobedience and unbelief?

Looking Inward

Take a moment to reflect on all that you've explored thus far in this study of 2 Kings 14—17 and 2 Chronicles 25—28. Review your notes and answers, and think about how each of these things matters in your life today.

Tips for Small Groups: To get the most out of this section, form pairs or trios and have group members take turns answering these questions. Be honest and as open as you can in this discussion, but most of all, be encouraging and supportive of others. Be sensitive to those who are going through particularly difficult times, and don't press for people to speak if they're uncomfortable doing so.

11. Describe a time when you were frustrated because of poor leadership. How did you deal with that situation? What are some godly ways to address a problem of ungodly or misguided leadership in the church?

12. Have you ever been tempted to compromise your beliefs for the sake of peace or personal gain? Explain. How did that situation turn out? In what ways can compromise have a negative impact on your relationship with God?

13. Do you feel closer to God during times of prosperity or times of lack? What are the risks of losing sight of God during times of prosperity? What are the dangers of falling away from God during times of need? How can

you reach a better point of devotion in your relationship with God no matter what your situation?

Going Forward

14. Think of one or two things you have learned that you'd like to work on in the coming week. Remember that this is all about quality, not quantity. It's better to work on one specific area of life and do it well than to work on many and do poorly (or to be so overwhelmed that you simply don't try).

Do you want to reject the temptation to compromise your faith? Be specific. Go back through 2 Kings 14—17 and 2 Chronicles 25—28 and put a star next to the phrase or verse that is most encouraging to you. Consider memorizing that verse.

Real-Life Application Ideas: The book of 2 Kings is packed with stories of bad and evil leaders, but there are a few good ones as well. This week, take time to identify "good leaders" who have had a positive influence on your life. Then contact as many as you can to say thank you for the role they played. Ask each leader you thank for a tip on good leadership, then put those into practice wherever you play the role of leader.

Seeking Help

15. Write a prayer below (or simply pray one in silence), inviting God to work on your mind and heart in those areas you've noted in the Going Forward section. Be honest about your desires and fears.

Notes for Small Groups:

- *Look for ways to put into practice the things you wrote in the Going Forward section. Talk with other group members about your ideas, and commit to being accountable to one another.*
- *During the coming week, ask the Holy Spirit to continue to reveal truth to you from what you've read and studied.*
- *Before you start the next lesson, read 2 Kings 18—20 and 2 Chronicles 29—32. (See also Isa. 36—38.) For more in-depth lesson preparation, read chapters 10 and 11, "The Making of a King—Parts I and II," in Be Distinct.*

The Making of a King

(2 KINGS 18—20; 2 CHRONICLES 29—32)

Before you begin …
- *Pray for the Holy Spirit to reveal truth and wisdom as you go through this lesson.*
- *Read 2 Kings 18—20 and 2 Chronicles 29—32. (See also Isa. 36—38.) This lesson references chapters 10 and 11 in* Be Distinct. *It will be helpful for you to have your Bible and a copy of the commentary available as you work through this lesson.*

Getting Started

From the Commentary

In 2 Chronicles 29, we see that Hezekiah didn't waste any time getting Judah back to the worship of the true and living God. His father, Ahaz, had defiled the temple and finally closed the doors and stopped the Levitical ministry (28:24). Hezekiah commanded the priests to sanctify themselves so they would be able to cleanse the temple and restore the worship that the Lord had commanded through Moses. The abandoning of the temple worship by the people of the northern kingdom had led to their captivity, and the defiling and neglecting of the temple by Ahaz had brought discipline to Judah, including invasions by Syria, Edom, and Philistia. The temple worship was at the heart of the Jewish nation, and if that was wrong, everything else would be wrong.

But Hezekiah wasn't interested in a mere housecleaning project, because he had it in his heart not only to rededicate the temple and the people but also to enter into a covenant with the Lord (29:10).

—*Be Distinct*, page 162

1. Why did Hezekiah make it a priority to clean the temple? (See 2 Chron. 29:3–19.) How did cleaning the temple pave the way for a healthier nation? What does "temple cleaning" look like in today's church?

More to Consider: Fourteen leaders are named in 2 Chronicles 29:12–14, men who set the example and led the way for a new beginning for temple ministry. If the spiritual leaders aren't right with God, how can He bless His people? All three Levitical families were represented. The clan of Elizaphan belonged to the Kohathites (Num. 3:30) and had achieved an honorable reputation because of their faithful service. They were represented by Shimri and Jeiel. The other men listed were among the temple singers related to Asaph, Heman, or Jeduthun, well-known musicians, singers, and worship leaders. King Hezekiah knew that there had to be music and praise or the temple worship would displease the Lord. Why are these individuals named in this passage? Why did their individual contributions matter to God? What does the inclusion of musicians and singers tell us about God's plan for worship?

2. Choose one verse or phrase from 2 Kings 18—20 or 2 Chronicles 29—32 that stands out to you. This could be something you're intrigued by, something that makes you uncomfortable, something that puzzles you, something that resonates with you, or just something you want to examine further. Write that here.

Going Deeper

From the Commentary

The king and the rulers of the city met together at the temple and offered sacrifices to the Lord. They brought sacrifices for the kingdom (Judah and Israel), the temple, and the kingdom of Judah in particular. The sin offerings were offered to atone for the sins of the people, and the priests included both Israel and Judah (2 Chron. 29:24—"all Israel"). The burnt offerings symbolized total dedication to the Lord. As the sacrifices were being offered to the Lord, the musicians and singers offered their praise to the Lord, following David's instructions, using David's songs, and playing David's instruments (vv. 25–27, 30; 1 Chron. 23:5–6).

But this wasn't a dedication service planned only for the king and his leaders, for the people in the congregation sanctified themselves and brought their offerings as well (2 Chron. 29:28–36). They brought a large number of sacrifices, including three thousand sheep, which were probably given as fellowship offerings. Part of the fellowship offering was kept by the worshipper and eaten with his family as a fellowship meal. Hezekiah was following the example of Solomon when he dedicated the temple more than two hundred years before (1 Kings 8:62ff.). It was a time of great rejoicing for the king and his people. Keep in mind that many devout people from the apostate northern kingdom of Israel (now Samaria) had fled to Judah so they could worship the Lord according to the law of Moses, so this dedication service involved all the tribes.

—*Be Distinct*, page 164

3. Why was it important that the dedication service involve the whole congregation and not just the leaders? What does this teach us about God's plan for His people even in the time of the kings? How does it speak to the exclusivity and the inclusivity of God's kingdom?

From the Commentary

Judah had been a vassal state under Assyria since the reign of King Ahaz, Hezekiah's father (2 Kings 16:7–18). When Sargon, ruler of Assyria, died in battle, and Sennacherib took the throne, it seemed to Hezekiah an opportune time to break that yoke. Sennacherib was involved in other empire concerns, so Hezekiah didn't send him the annual tribute. Judah had been victorious over the Philistines, so the kingdom was feeling strong. In 722 BC, Assyria attacked Israel and captured the city of

Samaria, and this meant that the Assyrian army was now right next door to Judah.

In 715 BC, Sennacherib invaded Judah and headed toward Jerusalem. Hezekiah's faith was very weak, so he humbled himself before the king and paid the tribute money that he owed—eleven tons of silver and one ton of gold. Some of the wealth came from the king's own treasure, but it's disappointing to see that Hezekiah took the rest of it from the temple of the Lord. He followed the bad example of his father (16:8). King David didn't negotiate with his enemies or try to buy them off; he attacked and defeated them. Of course, Sennacherib withdrew from Judah, but he had every intention of returning.

—*Be Distinct*, page 168

4. Review 2 Kings 18:7–16. What does this passage show about Hezekiah's leadership abilities? Why would he take from the temple treasure to pay the rest of the tribute to Sennacherib? What does this say about his character? How are his choices here similar to some of the scandals in the modern church?

From the Commentary

According to the chronologers, 2 Kings 20:1–11; 2 Chronicles 32:24–26; and Isaiah 38:1–8 record the next important event in the life of Hezekiah. It took place fifteen years before his death in 687 BC, so his sickness and healing, as well as the visit of the Babylonian ambassadors, occurred in the year 702. The next year, the Assyrians returned and attacked Jerusalem.

Did the Lord send this sickness to discipline Hezekiah because he compromised with the Assyrians? The record in 2 Chronicles 32:24–25 tells us that the king had become proud, and this was one way that the Lord humbled him. The fact that the prophet Isaiah visited him with such a solemn message indicates how serious this experience really was, for the king was going to die. "Set your house in order" involved most of all appointing an heir to the throne. Hezekiah had become king at the age of twenty-five (2 Kings 18:1–2) and died in 687 BC. His son Manasseh became king in 687 at the age of twenty-two, which means he was born in 709, so he would have been seven years old when Isaiah told his father he was going to die. Joash had ascended the throne at the age of seven (11:4ff.), but he had Jehoiada the godly priest to advise him.

—*Be Distinct*, page 169

5. Why was the throne of David in jeopardy? What was Hezekiah's response to falling ill? Is his statement in 2 Kings 20:3 and Isaiah 38:3 boasting? Why or why not? (See 2 Chron. 6:16–17.)

From the Commentary

The prophet Isaiah recorded the psalm Hezekiah wrote after he had been healed and given fifteen more years of life (Isa. 38:9–20). It's likely that Hezekiah wrote other psalms as well (see v. 20 KJV and NASB) because we read about "the men of Hezekiah" in Proverbs 25:1. This title suggests that the king had a special "guild" of scholars who worked with the Scriptures and copied the manuscripts. The psalm that Hezekiah wrote in commemoration of his sickness and deliverance certainly is filled with vivid imagery that teaches us a great deal about life and death. This is especially true in the NIV translation.

Hezekiah saw life as a journey that ended at the gates of death, or "Sheol," the Hebrew word for the realm of the dead (Isa. 38:10). He was in the prime of his life and yet was being robbed of the rest of his years. (He was probably thirty-seven or thirty-eight years old.) Perhaps he was thinking of Psalm 139:16, where David declares that God has written in His book the number of each person's days.

—*Be Distinct*, pages 170–71

6. What was Hezekiah's lament? What did it reveal about his understanding of life and death? How might his psalm have been different had he been privy to knowledge about eternal life as revealed in the New Testament (2 Tim. 1:10)?

From the Commentary

Scripture pictures our adversary the Devil as a serpent and a lion (Gen. 3:1ff.; 2 Cor. 11:1–4; 1 Peter 5:8–9). Satan usually comes first as a serpent to deceive us, but if that doesn't work, he returns as a lion to devour us. This was Hezekiah's experience. First the Babylonian ambassadors came to Jerusalem to learn how wealthy and strong Judah was, and then the Assyrian army came to ravage the land, capture Jerusalem, and deport the Jewish people to Assyria. The ambassadors deceived Hezekiah because he didn't seek God's wisdom from Isaiah the prophet, but the king did seek the Lord when the Assyrians invaded the land, and the Lord gave him victory.

We have already learned that Hezekiah had a problem with pride (2 Chron. 32:25–26). His near-fatal sickness did humble him, but the visit of the Babylonian envoys made it clear that the old sin was still very much alive.

—*Be Distinct*, pages 175–76

7. Review 2 Kings 20:12–13; 2 Chronicles 32:27–30; and Isaiah 39:1–2. How did Hezekiah's pride trip him up in this story? In what ways did Babylon come first as a serpent and then later as a lion? Why didn't Hezekiah take the initial threat from Babylon seriously? What can we learn from his errors as we face attacks on the church today?

From the Commentary

"After these deeds of faithfulness, Sennacherib king of Assyria came and entered Judah" (2 Chron. 32:1 NKJV). The "deeds of faithfulness" were Hezekiah's labors to cleanse and consecrate the temple, the priests, and the

Levites, and to restore true worship in Judah. One would think that God would reward his service by giving him peace, but instead, the Lord allowed the Assyrians to return to Judah and threaten Jerusalem.

—*Be Distinct*, page 178

8. It appears in this story that Hezekiah was faithful to the Lord but the Lord wasn't faithful to Hezekiah. Why didn't the Lord protect Judah from another invasion? What divine purposes did God have yet to fulfill in Hezekiah's life and in the life of the nation? What did the king need to learn? (See Josh. 5:13–15.)

More to Consider: The Assyrian army chose Lachish for their central camp, thirty miles southwest of Jerusalem, and brought a large army against Jerusalem. Three of the Assyrian officers told Hezekiah to send out three of his officers to arrange for the terms of surrender. Isaiah had predicted that the Assyrians would return, and they did. Once again, kings and leaders seemed to have missed the message God was giving them through His prophets. Why did the kings struggle so often to hear God? What are the obstacles we face today that keep us from hearing God?

From the Commentary

When the outlook is bleak, try the uplook. That's what King Hezekiah did when he received the blasphemous letter from the king of Assyria. Often in my own ministry, I have had to spread letters before the Lord and trust Him to work matters out, and He always has.

Hezekiah looked beyond his own throne and the throne of the "great king" Sennacherib and focused his attention on the throne of God who was "enthroned between the cherubim" (2 Kings 19:15; Isa. 37:16 NIV; see Ps. 80:1; 99:1). Since he was not a high priest, Hezekiah couldn't enter the Holy of Holies, where the mercy seat sat upon the ark of the covenant, but he could "enter" by faith even as believers can today (Heb. 10:19–25). At each end of the mercy seat was a cherub, and the mercy seat was the throne of God on earth (Ex. 25:10–22). Not only is the

Lord the King of Israel and the King of all nations, but He is the creator of the heavens and the earth.

—*Be Distinct*, page 184

9. Review 2 Kings 19:14–19; 2 Chronicles 32:20; and Isaiah 37:14–20. In what ways was Hezekiah lost in worship here? How does his worship exemplify how we ought to pray about life's problems? How does focusing on the Lord help put our problems in perspective?

From the Commentary

The Lord told Isaiah to get His message to the king, and the prophet obeyed. The answer to Hezekiah's prayer was threefold: (1) God would deliver Jerusalem, (2) God would defeat the Assyrian army and they would depart, and (3) God would care for the people and they would not starve. But God also had a message of rebuke to Sennacherib because of his pride and blasphemy.

—*Be Distinct*, page 185

10. Review 2 Kings 19:20–37; 2 Chronicles 32:20–22; and Isaiah 37:21–38. How was Hezekiah's faith rewarded? Why did God choose to answer Hezekiah's prayer? How did the message of rebuke to Sennacherib speak indirectly to the Jews who had struggled repeatedly to follow God?

Looking Inward

Take a moment to reflect on all that you've explored thus far in this study of 2 Kings 18—20 and 2 Chronicles 29—32. Review your notes and answers, and think about how each of these things matters in your life today.

Tips for Small Groups: To get the most out of this section, form pairs or trios and have group members take turns answering these questions. Be honest and as open as you can in this discussion, but most of all, be encouraging and supportive of others. Be sensitive to those who are going through particularly difficult times, and don't press for people to speak if they're uncomfortable doing so.

11. A "clean" temple was important for God's people in the time of the kings. What does a clean temple look like in your own life? How do you clean your spiritual temple?

12. Where do you feel most involved and included at church? Is it important for you to feel like a part of the leadership of a church? Why or why not? What are some of the ways your personal involvement in church makes you feel like part of God's greater plan for redemption?

13. Have you ever been in a situation in which you thought God rewarded the wrong person or didn't reward someone who did the right thing? Explain. How do you rationalize that thought? What might God have been doing behind the scenes in the lives of those involved?

Going Forward

14. Think of one or two things you have learned that you'd like to work on in the coming week. Remember that this is all about quality, not quantity. It's better to work on one specific area of life and do it well than to work on many and do poorly (or to be so overwhelmed that you simply don't try).

Do you want to humble yourself to avoid the consequences of pride? Be specific. Go back through 2 Kings 18—20 and 2 Chronicles 29—32 and put a star next to the phrase or verse that is most encouraging to you. Consider memorizing that verse.

Real-Life Application Ideas: This week, take a long look at your current involvement in your local church. What are the ways you're currently contributing to the life of the church? What are some ways you could become more involved? Keep in mind that the goal here isn't to overdo it but to find the best fit for your skills and gifts. Talk with trusted friends and counselors, and listen to their wisdom. Finding the best fit in a church not only benefits your relationship with God but also can benefit others.

Seeking Help

15. Write a prayer below (or simply pray one in silence), inviting God to work on your mind and heart in those areas you've noted in the Going Forward section. Be honest about your desires and fears.

Notes for Small Groups:

- *Look for ways to put into practice the things you wrote in the Going Forward section. Talk with other group members about your ideas, and commit to being accountable to one another.*

- *During the coming week, ask the Holy Spirit to continue to reveal truth to you from what you've read and studied.*

- *Before you start the next lesson, read 2 Kings 21—25 and 2 Chronicles 33—36. For more in-depth lesson preparation, read chapters 12 and 13, "The End Is Near" and "The End Has Come," in* Be Distinct.

The End
(2 KINGS 21—25; 2 CHRONICLES 33—36)

Before you begin ...
- *Pray for the Holy Spirit to reveal truth and wisdom as you go through this lesson.*
- *Read 2 Kings 21—25 and 2 Chronicles 33—36. This lesson references chapters 12 and 13 in* Be Distinct. *It will be helpful for you to have your Bible and a copy of the commentary available as you work through this lesson.*

Getting Started

From the Commentary

In 2 Kings 21—23 and 2 Chronicles 33—35, we study three kings—Manasseh, Amon, and Josiah. The Jewish nation had given the world a witness to the one true and living God, but now many of the people worshipped foreign idols. Israel gave the world the prophets and the Scriptures, but most of the leaders of Judah no longer listened to God's Word. Josiah was Judah's last good king.

The Lord had covenanted to protect David's throne so that the promised Redeemer might one day come, but now the government of Judah was decaying and the very existence of the kingdom was in jeopardy. The future of God's plan of redemption for a lost world rested with the faithful remnant that resisted the inroads of pagan culture and remained true to the Lord.

God's promise hadn't changed: "If my people, which are called by my name, shall humble themselves, and pray, and seek my face, and turn from their wicked ways; then will I hear from heaven, and will forgive their sin, and will heal their land" (2 Chron. 7:14).

—*Be Distinct*, pages 191–92

1. Why did each of these three kings have to learn about humility? Why is humility such a critical trait in leaders? How does humility strengthen a leader?

2. Choose one verse or phrase from 2 Kings 21—25 or 2 Chronicles 33—36 that stands out to you. This could be something you're intrigued by, something that makes you uncomfortable, something that puzzles you,

something that resonates with you, or just something you want to examine further. Write that here.

Going Deeper

From the Commentary

> That godly King Hezekiah should have such a wicked son is another one of those puzzles in biblical history. If Manasseh was born in 709 BC, then he was seven years old when his father was healed and the miracle of the shadow occurred. He was eight years old when the 185,000 Assyrian soldiers were slain. Apparently these miracles made little impression on his heart. Many scholars think that Manasseh was coregent with his father for perhaps ten years (697–687), from age twelve to twenty-two, and the son lived in close relationship with a godly father. But the remarkable thing is that Manasseh became the most wicked king in Judah's history, so much so that he is blamed for the fall of the southern kingdom (2 Kings 24:3; Jer. 15:1–4).
>
> —*Be Distinct*, page 192

3. Review 2 Kings 21:1–16 and 2 Chronicles 33:1–10. What are some of the ways Manasseh was wicked? Why would such wickedness come from a man who might have served as coregent to such a godly king? What does this teach us about the pervasiveness of sin?

More to Consider: The word "forsake" in 2 Kings 21:14 means "to give over to judgment." God promised never to abandon His people (1 Sam. 12:22; 2 Sam. 7:23–24), but He also warned that He would chasten them if they disobeyed Him. How did God chasten His people in this chapter of history? How was God being faithful to His covenant in both blessing and chastening? Why is this significant in understanding God's Old Testament character?

From the Commentary

The writer of 2 Kings wrote nothing about the remarkable change in Manasseh's life, but we find the record in 2 Chronicles. Apparently he displeased the king of Assyria in some way, and God allowed the Assyrian officers to come to Judah and capture the king. This was no respectable act of taking somebody into custody, because they put a hook in his nose and bound him with chains (2 Chron. 33:11 NIV). He was treated like a steer being led to the slaughter, and he deserved it. The city of Babylon was a second capital for Assyria at that time, and there they imprisoned him.

The whole experience was one of great humiliation for this wicked king, and the Lord used it to chasten him, break his pride, and bring him to his knees. He prayed to the Lord for forgiveness, and the Lord kept His promise and forgave him (2 Chron. 7:14). Even more, the Lord moved the Assyrians to set him free and allow him to return to Jerusalem to rule over the people. What a trophy of the grace of God!

When he returned home, Manasseh proved the reality of his conversion by seeking to undo all the evil he had done. He fortified Jerusalem and other cities in Judah, he removed his idol from the temple (33:7, 15), and he removed from the temple all the altars he had put up to false gods. Having purged the temple, he then repaired the altar of the Lord that had been neglected, and he offered thank offerings to the Lord who had rescued him. He commanded the people of Judah to serve the Lord, and he set the example. He allowed them to offer sacrifices in the high places, but not to pagan gods—only to the God of Israel. "Therefore bear fruit in keeping with repentance," John the Baptist told the Pharisees and Sadducees (Matt. 3:8 NASB), and that's exactly what Manasseh did.

—*Be Distinct*, pages 194–95

4. Manasseh humbled himself (2 Chron. 33:12), but the Lord first humbled him (v. 19). What does this reveal to us about the nature of true repentance? How did Manasseh's actions prove his repentance was sincere?

From the Commentary

After his repentance, Manasseh tried to undo all the damage he had done to Jerusalem and Judah, but there was one place where he could make no changes—in the heart of his son Amon. The young man had been too influenced by his father's sins to take notice of his new life of obedience, and there were, no doubt, people at court who encouraged Amon to maintain the old ways. Whereas Manasseh humbled himself before the Lord, his son Amon refused to do so (2 Chron. 33:23), and the longer he sinned, the harder his heart became.

"The wages of sin is death" (Rom. 6:23). Why Amon's own officials should assassinate him isn't made clear, but the reason probably wasn't spiritual. While it's true that the law of Moses declared that idolaters should be slain (Deut. 13), there was nobody in the land with the authority to deal with an idolatrous king. It's likely that the conspirators were more interested in politics. Amon was probably pro-Assyrian—after all, they had released his father from prison—while the officials were pro-Babylonian, not realizing that the rise of Babylon would ultimately mean the fall of Judah. Amon's son Josiah was definitely pro-Babylonian and even lost his life on the battlefield trying to stop the Egyptian army from assisting Assyria against Babylon. The fact that the people made Josiah the next king would suggest that they didn't want a pro-Assyria king.

—*Be Distinct*, pages 195–96

5. Why didn't Manasseh's repentance trickle down to his son? What kept Amon from a similar repentance? How might Amon's story have been different had he listened to his father and learned from his mistakes? What does this story teach us about the importance of humility?

From the Commentary

Out of the twenty rulers of Judah, including wicked Queen Athaliah, only eight of them could be called "good":

Asa, Jehoshaphat, Joash, Amaziah, Uzziah, Jotham, Hezekiah, and Josiah. There's no question that Josiah was a great king, for even the prophet Jeremiah used him as an example for the other rulers to follow. "He pled the cause of the afflicted and needy," said Jeremiah of Josiah, while the kings that followed Josiah exploited the people so they could build their elaborate palaces (Jer. 22:11–17 NASB). Josiah ruled for thirty-one years (640–609 BC) and walked in the ways of the Lord because David was his model. No doubt his mother was a godly woman and guided her son wisely. He was only eight years old when they made him king, so the court officials were his mentors, but at age sixteen, Josiah committed himself to the Lord and began to seek His blessing.

—*Be Distinct*, page 196

6. Josiah ruled during a time when Assyria was on the decline and Babylon hadn't yet reached its zenith. How might that have played into his success as a leader? How did the people respond to this season of relative peace and safety?

From the Commentary

King Josiah was a godly man who sincerely wanted to serve the Lord, but he made a foolish blunder by attacking Pharaoh Neco (Necho). His meddling in Egypt's affairs was a personal political decision and not a command from the Lord. Josiah wanted to prevent Pharaoh Neco from assisting Assyria in their fight against Babylon, little realizing that it was Babylon and not Assyria that would be Judah's greatest enemy. Josiah was mortally wounded by an arrow at Megiddo and died in Jerusalem. With the death of Josiah, the kingdom of Judah lost her independence and became subject to Egypt. This lasted from 609 to about 606 BC, and then Egypt retreated and Babylon took over.

According to 1 Chronicles 3:15–16, Josiah had four sons: Johanan; Eliakim, who was renamed Jehoiakim; Mattaniah, who was renamed Zedekiah; and Shallum, also known as Jehoahaz. We know nothing about Johanan and assume he died in childhood. When Josiah died, the people put Josiah's youngest son, Jehoahaz, on the throne and bypassed the other two brothers. His given name was Shallum (Jer. 22:11) and Jehoahaz was the name he was given when he took the throne. Jehoahaz and Zedekiah were full brothers (2 Kings 23:31; 24:18). It's obvious that the Jeremiah mentioned in 23:31 isn't the prophet Jeremiah, since the prophet was unmarried (Jer. 16:1–2).

Jehoahaz reigned only three months. When Neco was returning to Egypt with his army, he deposed Jehoahaz, made Eliakim king, renaming him Jehoiakim, and placed a heavy tax on the land. It's likely that Jehoiakim was pro-Egypt in politics while Jehoahaz favored alliances with Babylon, as had his father, Josiah. Pharaoh met Jehoahaz at the Egyptian military headquarters at Riblah and from there took him to Egypt where Jehoahaz died. The prophet Jeremiah had predicted this event. He told the people not to mourn the death of Josiah, but rather to mourn the exile of his son and successor, Shallum, for he would never see Judah again (Jer. 22:10–12). But unlike his godly father, Josiah, Jehoahaz was an ungodly man and an evil king and deserved to be exiled.

—*Be Distinct*, pages 207–8

7. Review 2 Kings 23:29–33 and 2 Chronicles 35:20—36:4. How did politics get in the way of obedience to God? How does this happen in the modern church? How can church leaders avoid making the same mistake Josiah did?

From the Commentary

Having deposed Jehoahaz, Pharaoh Neco selected Josiah's second son to be the next regent, changing his name from Eliakim to Jehoiakim. Both names mean "God has established," but the new name used the covenant name "Jehovah" in place of "El," the common name for God. By doing this, Neco was claiming to be the Lord's agent in ruling Judah. Of course, the new king had to swear allegiance to Neco in the name of Jehovah, and his new name would remind him of his obligations. In order to pay tribute to Neco, the new king taxed the people of the land. He reigned for eleven years, and during that time, Judah got more and more in trouble with the surrounding nations.

—*Be Distinct*, page 209

8. In what ways was Jehoiakim a wicked man? (See Jer. 22:1–23; 26:20–24.) What was Jeremiah's opinion of the king? (See 22:18–19.) What does Jehoiakim's story, like so many others, teach us about the importance of having respect for the Lord and His Word?

More to Consider: The scenario of King Jehoiakim's death must be put together from information given in the books of 2 Kings, 2 Chronicles, and Jeremiah. In 597 BC, Nebuchadnezzar came to Jerusalem to punish the rebellious king; but before he arrived, his officers had captured Jehoiakim and bound him to take him prisoner to Babylon (2 Chron. 36:5–6). We aren't told whether he died a natural death or was killed (2 Kings 24:6); the verse briefly mentions only his death ("slept with his fathers"). He died in December 598, before Nebuchadnezzar arrived on the scene in March 597 (2 Kings 24:10ff.). How did Jehoiakim's imprisonment and death match up with his way of living? This doesn't always happen in biblical history. Sometimes evil seems to "win" while good pays a price. What can we learn about the nature of God when evil people suffer? What can we learn about God when good people suffer?

From the Commentary

In 605 BC, during the reign of Jehoiakim, the Babylonians had deported some of Judah's best young men to Babylon to be trained for official duty, among them Daniel and his three friends (Dan. 1:1–6). The second deportation was in 597 (2 Kings 24:10–16), when over ten thousand people were sent to Babylon. But Zedekiah, Jehoiakim's successor, still favored getting help from Egypt, and in 588, the political situation seemed just right for Zedekiah to revolt against Babylon (2 Kings 24:20; 2 Chron. 36:13). Nebuchadnezzar responded by marching his army to Jerusalem, but when the Egyptian army moved to help King Zedekiah, the Babylonians withdrew temporarily to face Egypt. Nebuchadnezzar knew it was unwise to fight a war on two fronts. God sent Jeremiah to warn Zedekiah that Nebuchadnezzar would return (Jer. 37), but Zedekiah's faith was in Egypt, not in the Lord (Ezek. 17:11–21). Zedekiah even called an "international conference" involving Edom, Moab, Ammon, Tyre, and Sidon (Jer. 27), hoping that these nations would work together to keep Babylon at bay. However, Nebuchadnezzar stopped Egypt and then returned to Jerusalem and the punishment of Zedekiah.

The siege of Jerusalem began on January 15, 588 BC, and continued until July 18, 586.

—Be Distinct, pages 212–13

9. Review 2 Kings 24:18—25:21 and 2 Chronicles 36:11–21. In what ways did Jeremiah's prophecy come true (Jer. 34:1–7; see also chapters 39 and 52)? After removing everything valuable from the city and the temple, the Babylonians finished breaking down the walls of the city and set fire to Jerusalem and the temple. Why did God allow the destruction of the city and temple? (See 2 Chron. 36:14–16; Lam. 4:13; Ezek. 8—9.) What does this chapter in biblical history teach us about obeying God?

From the Commentary

As we come to the close of this record of the tragic decline and destruction of a great nation, we need to take some lessons to heart. *No nation rises any higher than its worship of God.* The nation of Israel was torn into two kingdoms because of the sins of Solomon, who turned to idols in order to please his pagan wives. Because they worshipped idols and forsook the true God, the northern kingdom of Israel was taken captive by Assyria. It didn't take long for Judah to succumb and eventually be captured by Babylon. We become like the god we worship (Ps. 115:8), and if we refuse to worship the true and living God, we become as helpless as the idols that enthrall us.

At this critical time in history, God is seeking dedicated, distinctive people—not cookie-cutter, carbon-copy Christians. Friendship with the world is enmity with God (James 4:4), and to love the world and trust it is to lose the love of the Father (1 John 2:15–17). We are to be "living sacrifices" for the Lord (Rom. 12:1–2), distinctive people whose lives and witness point to Christ and shine like lights in the darkness. "A city that is set on a hill cannot be hid" (Matt. 5:14). Faith is living without scheming. Start to explain away the clear teachings of the Bible about obedience to the Lord and separation from sin, and you will soon find yourself sliding gradually out of the light and into the shadows and then into the darkness, eventually ending in shame and defeat.

—*Be Distinct*, pages 217–18

10. In what ways were the people who led astray Israel and Judah conformers? Whom did they most want to please? How did God warn them of their folly? What was their response to these warnings? Is God warning the modern church of folly? Explain.

Looking Inward

Take a moment to reflect on all that you've explored thus far in this study of 2 Kings 21—25 and 2 Chronicles 33—36. Review your notes and answers, and think about how each of these things matters in your life today.

> *Tips for Small Groups: To get the most out of this section, form pairs or trios and have group members take turns answering these questions. Be honest and as open as you can in this discussion, but most of all, be encouraging and supportive of others. Be sensitive to those who are going through particularly difficult times, and don't press for people to speak if they're uncomfortable doing so.*

11. Did you ever rebel against your parents? What prompted that rebellion? If that rebellion took you away from God, what brought you back? How has the faith of those who have gone before you (whether family or friends)

formed the person you have become? What are some ways you can honor the faithfulness of others?

12. How do you juggle your politics and faith? Have you ever been temped to change or compromise your faith for the benefit of some political gain? What do you do when your politics and faith don't agree? How do you live out your faith in light of a political climate you may not agree with?

13. The kings and leaders who got the Jews into the most trouble were conformers. What are some of the ways you're tempted to conform to the world? How do you fight against that temptation? In what ways does following God make you a bit of a rebel? How can you use that rebellion to further God's kingdom?

Going Forward

14. Think of one or two things you have learned that you'd like to work on in the coming week. Remember that this is all about quality, not quantity. It's better to work on one specific area of life and do it well than to work on many and do poorly (or to be so overwhelmed that you simply don't try).

Do you want to become better at avoiding the temptation to conform? Be specific. Go back through 2 Kings 21—25 and 2 Chronicles 33—36 and put a star next to the phrase or verse that is most encouraging to you. Consider memorizing that verse.

Real-Life Application Ideas: One of the big themes in this section of 2 Kings is that of humbling yourself before God. Unlike what the world sometimes preaches, humility isn't the same thing as weakness. True humility is a position of strength because it counts on God's power, not our own. This week, take time to learn what it really means to be humble before God. Do a word study of humility and talk about the topic with friends, family members, and church leaders. Then put into practice all that you learn.

Seeking Help

15. Write a prayer below (or simply pray one in silence), inviting God to work on your mind and heart in those areas you've noted in the Going Forward section. Be honest about your desires and fears.

Notes for Small Groups:

- *Look for ways to put into practice the things you wrote in the Going Forward section. Talk with other group members about your ideas, and commit to being accountable to one another.*
- *During the coming week, ask the Holy Spirit to continue to reveal truth to you from what you've read and studied.*

Summary and Review

Notes for Small Groups: This session is a summary and review of this book. Because of that, it is shorter than the previous lessons. If you are using this in a small-group setting, consider combining this lesson with a time of fellowship or a shared meal.

Before you begin ...
- *Pray for the Holy Spirit to reveal truth and wisdom as you go through this lesson.*
- *Briefly review the notes you made in the previous sessions. You will refer back to previous sections throughout this bonus lesson.*

Looking Back

1. Over the past eight lessons, you've examined 2 Kings (and 2 Chronicles). What expectations did you bring to this study? In what ways were those expectations met?

2. What is the most significant personal discovery you've made from this study?

3. What surprised you most about 2 Kings? What, if anything, troubled you?

Progress Report

4. Take a few moments to review the Going Forward sections of the previous lessons. How would you rate your progress for each of the things you chose to work on? What adjustments, if any, do you need to make to continue on the path toward spiritual maturity?

5. In what ways have you grown closer to Christ during this study? Take a moment to celebrate those things. Then think of areas where you feel you still need to grow and note those here. Make plans to revisit this study in a few weeks to review your growing faith.

Things to Pray About

6. Second Kings is a book about trusting God despite what the world says—it's about owning the distinctiveness that comes from following God. As you reflect on this theme, ask God to help you be bold in your faith.

7. The topics in 2 Kings include obedience, trusting God's truth, listening to God, owning your faith, and humility. Spend time praying about each of these topics.

8. Whether you've been studying this in a small group or on your own, there are many other Christians working through the very same issues you discovered when examining 2 Kings. Take time to pray for them, that God would reveal truth, that the Holy Spirit would guide you, and that each person might grow in spiritual maturity according to God's will.

A Blessing of Encouragement

Studying the Bible is one of the best ways to learn how to be more like Christ. Thanks for taking this step. In closing, let this blessing precede you and follow you into the next week while you continue to marinate in God's Word:

May God light your path to greater understanding as you review the truths found in 2 Kings and 2 Chronicles and consider how they can help you grow closer to Christ.